Manif Money

Amanda Rose

amanda@amandarosefitness.com

Cover by Daniel McCutcheon

1st Edition

Dedication

To you, and the incredible journey you have ahead.

INTRODUCTION

Oh, money.

What a hot topic.

It's loaded; like sex, politics, or religion. It's become taboo to talk about. It's really a wonder most people have any at all with how *dirty* the societal view of money is and all the hang-ups we create around it.

Yet here you are. You picked up this book because I presume, you want some more of the green stuff (or, you know, if you're Canadian like me more of the multi-colored "monopoly" bills). Either way, you're tired of where your finances are at and are ready for an upgrade in the bank account department.

I, like most people, used to think of finances as an external thing. I thought rich successful people had some sort of secret, and if I could just learn that secret, I could be wealthy too. I assumed it would be something hard, and I was down for that disco, ready to take on the challenge, put in some elbow grease, and get 'er done.

I. Was. Wrong.

There was something I didn't know, but it wasn't what I had expected. What needed to be changed and worked on wasn't what I was *doing*, it was what I was *thinking*. Now, I'd heard about, and even grown up with, the *Law of Attraction* in my household. It was a concept I was aware of. However, in my teens and early adulthood, the many adult tasks thrust upon me put the responsibility and reality of being a grown-up squarely on my shoulders, and the law of attraction and mindset practices I once did daily fell to the wayside.

When the idea of focusing on personal development came up in my life as the area I needed to focus on I resisted it. It took time, and some real poop hitting the fan, for me to get over my, "I already *know* that stuff," snobby attitude, and to change it to, "I'm ready and willing to learn, please teach me, I am SO done with the struggling!"

And you know what? Surprise, surprise.... My life began to change! And it changed *fast.*

THE UNIVERSE CAN WORK

INSTANTANEOUSLY

ONCE WE'RE READY

Your life can change in the blink of an eye too. Whether you want to start your own business, get debt free, live out a lifelong dream, take your family on exotic vacations, buy the dream home, get the sports car, donate to your favorite charities – whatever you want to do, money is the conduit to make it your reality. The way to make it happen all starts in your mind.

In this book we're going to work through understanding what money really is, uprooting deep seeded unsupportive beliefs about money, get clear on what you really want money for, and how to manifest money into your life.

Money Ain't the Bad Guy Here

Money gets a bad rap. Somewhere along the way, we decided to start blaming money for... pretty much everything. But really, what did money ever do to anyone that's made it so bad? I don't know about you, but money has never tripped me down the stairs, kicked me in the shin, punched me in the throat, or stolen from me. In fact, money hasn't really done anything. It's inert, an inanimate object, no different from a chair, table, or desk.

Money is a Blank Slate

Neither inherently Good or Evil

WHAT IS MONEY?

Money is the conduit to how we make things happen. Money in and of itself is simply a form of exchange. Before money, we had to barter and trade for the things and services we wanted and needed. You build me a fence, I give you a goat – that kind of thing. But trading goats for fences is a pain, and what if my fence maker doesn't want a goat? So, we smart human beings developed currency and assigned it value – which when you think about it basically makes money an I.O.U. for the things you want so you don't get stuck with another goat. *Bahhh!*

Money Becomes

What We Have Assigned it to be

We, society, decide what money is worth. That value changes slowly over time, with inflation, as the numbers jumble around, but all in all, we understand these numbers and their exchange value in terms of the goods and services the money can buy. It's our method of exchange, pure and simple.

WHY THE HATE?

So, what's with the mistrust, fear, and anger towards money? It's complicated. Our relationship with money isn't as simple as it should be, and that's where our work begins. Once we understand why we feel the way we do about money, we can change the relationship and welcome money with open arms into our lives.

On the surface, we all want more money. Ask just about anyone if they'd like a million dollars to fall into their lap and you'll get a resounding, "Uh, yes! Duh!" But deep down, below the surface, that's not the case.

YOUR SUBCONSCIOUS RULES SURPEME

Consciously, we can talk about how we want and welcome money all day long, but if our subconscious ain't on board, then it isn't happening. Our subconscious mind is where our core beliefs live. Those beliefs dictate what you manifest into your life; our beliefs create our thoughts, our thoughts lead to our actions, and our actions lead to our results.

When we're creating our impression of the world, particularly in our youth between birth and about age 8, we have no filter. Our minds at that time haven't developed enough to decipher the information we received, so we accepted it all as truth and broke it down into simplest terms. Those "truths" about the world became our belief foundation, from which we use to base our decisions. Depending on the associations we made during those years, we may have a lot of helpful beliefs, or a lot of unhelpful... *please... go away*, ones.

These beliefs, as children, helped us to make sense of the world. As children we're vulnerable and we need the adults in our lives to look after us – and that means that we need to be *loved*. Quite simply, anything that would jeopardize our perceived ability to be loved, and therefore taken care of, we'd learn to push away. So, if the adults in your life when you were a child argued or fought about money, it's quite likely your subconscious mind made the association: money = fighting = if I have money I can't be loved.

Add onto this survival instinct-based reasoning all of the many things and sayings we hear about money growing up, that to an unfiltered mind, are accepted as truths:

- Money is the root of all evil

- Money corrupts
- Money doesn't grow on trees
- Money can't buy happiness
- Rich people oppress the poor
- Love is more important than money
- Having too much money makes you greedy
- Wealthy people are all snobs
- There's a never enough money
- You have to work hard for money
- Money turns good people into bad people

Then as adults, we have all of this information crammed into our subconscious mind. The way we think and feel about money has followed us around without being reexamined. So, while we're talking about how, "Dammit, I'm tired of scraping by, I want some freaking money!" our subconscious is still steering the car saying, "No, no we don't. Money is bad."

Now before you get all pissed off at your subconscious, remember:

Your Subconscious Wants to

Keep You Safe

Your subconscious mind is your pal, he was just looking out for you, and is merely acting out of fear. The subconscious is like a scared kid; we need to help this kid to see a new reality and way of being. So, buckle your seatbelt. It's time for you to start steering this car where you want it to go, and for that, we have to re-program your subconscious beliefs...

CHAPTER 1: BELIEFS

I think one of the most liberating things I learned when I dove wholeheartedly into personal development and law of attraction was that our beliefs, which most of us consider to be who we are, are changeable. What we consider to be "true" isn't a hard fact; we can choose to reprogram our minds at any time. The human experience is subjective and limited, based on our perceptions.

We Only Experience a Small Portion of Our reality

Our vantage point colors our beliefs about what is and isn't possible. Think about your senses, touch, taste, sight, scent, and hearing; these are the means by which we experience life. But we know in the animal kingdom there are animals that have better, and worse, senses than we do. Imagine how different your perception of life would be if you...

- Could see something as small as a mouse from 15,000 feet away like a buzzard can
- Could see clearly in the dark like a cat

- Could hear between 3000 and 120,000 Hz like a bat (Humans can hear 20 to 20,000 Hz but our primary range is just 1,000 to 5,000 – that's a far cry from what a bat can hear!)
- Could taste like a catfish who has 100,000 taste buds (humans only have roughly 10,000)
- Could smell like a dog whose olfactory membrane can sense 150+ sq. cm (Humans, by comparison, can only sense 5-10 sq. cm)
- Could fly like a bird
- Could breathe underwater like a fish

I could go on, but you get the point – our senses are limited, and our experiences are impacted by these limited senses. Knowing this, we can move forward aware that there are things beyond our perception.

Beyond the physical, there is this big old non-physical dimension that's just as important to consider. Your sixth sense, the one in tune with this non-physical plane of existence, is just as important as your 5 physical senses, and just as limited in perceiving. This is why most people only focus on the physical world; it's all that we can clearly perceive, albeit still in a limited way.

This is why it's so important to keep an open mind. We don't know everything. We live on one planet, in a small corner of a Universe that's so grand in scope we can't comprehend it fully. Our small, little, itty bitty, perception of what life is, isn't all there is to it.

Your Current Beliefs Aren't Carved in Stone

TIME TO TAKE A CLOSER LOOK

The first step we need to take on this transformative journey is to take a look into your beliefs and to see which ones serve who you want to become and which ones need to be let go of in order for you to grow. So, grab a piece of paper and a pen, and let's explore how you really feel about money…

TASK #1: Programming

What we learned about money growing up is what we were programmed with. How we interpreted that programming became our beliefs. Think back to your childhood, and answer the following:

1. When money was discussed by my parents/guardians, how was it talked about? How did it make me feel?
2. What common sayings did my parents/guardians use regarding money? List them all.
3. Were there any significant events in my household around money when I was growing up? How did they make me feel?
4. Growing up, with adults providing for me, did I feel taken care of, or like there was never enough?

TASK #2: What did money mean to your family?

Money means something different to every one of us. Reflecting on your parents/guardians, what do you think money represented to each of them? Thinking about their actions around money, review the list below and see which words you think match their behavior and attitude around money:

- Safety
- Freedom
- Fun
- Security
- Power

- Choice
- Happiness
- Instant Gratification
- Fulfillment
- Escapism

Example 1: Your father always wanted to save money, not spend it. Having enough money saved up symbolized freedom to him.

Example 2: Your mother loved to spend extra money whenever it came in. For her money symbolized instant gratification.

TASK #3: What does money mean to you?

Quite often we rebel against our parent/guardian's habits around money. Using Example 1 above, with the father that always saves money, and doesn't spend it, as we grew up we might have viewed this behavior as being a 'cheapskate' and vowed never to be so stingy around money ourselves, therefore overspending as an adult to compensate. Other times, we can pick up and mimic the habits of our parents/guardians.

Sometimes our mimicking or rebelling can work in our favor. Let's say, for example, Jane Doe's family was always broke, her father could barely scrape together rent, and made poor financial choices. That could have inspired her to be smart with her money, to learn about investing, and to always have a minimum balance in her bank account.

However, it doesn't matter if you're mimicking or rebelling, this behavior needs some examining...

- Look over the list above and see which of the words resonate about how you feel about money
- Think about how your parents/guardians were with money vs. how you are with money; do you see a pattern of behavior, either mimicking or rebelling (doing the opposite), what your parents/guardians did with money?
- How are your habits around money serving you?
- Which habits or patterns around money are holding you back?
- Which habits, if any, serve to help you to become who you want to be and the money you want to make?

Getting clear on how we view money, and why we treat it the way we do, helps us to release any unhelpful habits we've picked up.

TASK #4: Releasing

Once we have insight into our own money beliefs and patterns, we can let go of the ones that we picked up that do not serve us. It is important that we do this with love and compassion, instead of anger. It's easy to slip into the blame game, to get made at our upbringing or at our subconscious for twisting things in our head, but that's not the point. This is a natural part of the human journey of personal growth, it's nobody's fault, and your subconscious adapted its beliefs in an attempt to love and protect you.

As you move through releasing these old beliefs, try phrasing it along these lines:

"I no longer choose to believe ______________________. I realize that I misinterpreted a situation and adapted this belief as a means of survival. I now know that this is not the truth; it is not my truth. I am letting go of __________________________ and instead I choose to believe ___(Reprogramming)___"

TASK #5: Reprogramming

We are creatures of habit. Trying to simply stop a habit almost never works, however, swapping a bad habit for a good one is something we adapt to easily. This is what we are going to do. As we release our old beliefs, we'll be implanting new ones to replace them.

Quite often the easiest way to reprogram our beliefs is to flip them around. Rephrasing them in a new and empowering way can uplift us and give us the wind beneath our capes to be superhero manifesting badasses! So, let's take a few examples and flip them...

Old Belief: If I have money I won't be lovable

New Belief: I can have money AND love

Old Belief: If I have money I will be a bad person

New Belief: Money empowers me to be the best version of myself

Old Belief: People are more important than money

New Belief: Money gives me more time and freedom to be with the people I love

Old Belief: If I have money then all the people in my life will only want me for my money

New Belief: I attract people into my life who love me for who I am and not for my money

Old Belief: I'm not smart enough to deal with a lot of money

New Belief: I'm dedicated to learning about what to do with money so as I get more of it I know exactly what to do with it

Take at least 5 limiting beliefs you have and rephrase them in a way that empowers you. You'll use the new belief statement from each as an affirmation daily. By reminding yourself of this new belief daily it will become your default belief about money.

Wealth Builder To-do List:

- When you're embarking on any new task remember to remind yourself that your perception is limited. Trust the Universe knows all the details and moving parts that you cannot see and will guide you *if* you let it.
- Go through Tasks 1 through 5 to uncover your current money beliefs and to create new ones that support who you want to become
- Write down your 5 (or more) new beliefs and at least once a day read through them to implant those new beliefs in your subconscious mind.
- Say out loud and proud: *I am a Money Magnet!*

CHAPTER 2: CHOICE

In my mid-teenage years, I was leaning more and more into the arts and becoming an actor. I had amazing grades across the board, but I loved films and music and had always dreamed about being a movie star. As I made my decision to go into the artistic field I started to pick up some crappy hang-ups around money. Everyone and their uncle were spouting out things at me like...

- "What's your backup plan?"
- "What are you going to do to pay the bills?"
- "What's your day job going to be?"
- "Artists don't get paid much."
- "It's hard to get paying work as an actor."

And so on, and so on, and so on... *yawn*.

I was thoroughly unamused by these comments, but over time, they got stuck in my head. I started saying things like, "I don't care if I have to live in a cardboard box, I'd rather be an actor," and, "I'd crawl through raw sewage to be an actor." Ew.

I also got really disgusted with consumerism and with the idea of working a job that was soul-crushing just to pay the bills. The "American Dream" idea made me want to vomit and rebel. I thought people who were all about making money were gross and shallow, and wasting their lives. I hated money (sorry money, it wasn't your fault) and what people would do to make it, and so.... you guessed it, I was broke.

The truth of the matter had alluded me. It was ridiculous too because to be the big-name actor and artist I wanted to be, I'd, um... you know, get paid a lot! But I was pushing money away subconsciously because of my 'better than it' attitude. Because I was pushing money away I didn't have the money or the amazing artistic career!

My disdain for wealth was ironic to me once I began working on my wealth mindset because growing up I always imagined myself as a Hollywood movie star multi-millionaire. I imagined myself surrounded by wealth, in a big mansion, while doing what I loved. It wasn't an 'either or' situation. I could have BOTH.

The Universe Wants You To Have Everything You Need To Grow and Flourish

CHOOSE BOTH

You get what you decide on. Remember the Law of Attraction? Thoughts become things, it's literally your choice, so why not choose both?

- You can work your dream job AND have time with your loved ones
- You can be in an amazing relationship AND still have time for your favorite hobbies
- You can lose weight AND still have carbs
- You can be spiritual AND rich

This is a good time to bring up the "_____ is more important than money," discussion. I think this happens as a fear response, as one of our deep seeded excuses not to just freaking go for it! So, if in the back of your mind while you've been reading this book you've been thinking that family, being a good person, charity, inner growth, or fill in the freaking blank, is more important than money… YES, those things are important!

But… what the heck does that have to do with making money? You can make money AND have/do those things. And with money, you can do those meaningful things more often without being distracted with stressful thoughts about how to make ends meet this month.

Money is the Means To an End

Making money for money's sake is fairly meaningless. Money isn't the end game; money is what we use to be, do, or have more of the things we want. That's the entire plethora of what life have to offer.

Another massive hang-up the majority of people have is about who they will become once they have money. There's this belief, or rather a myth, that if you get rich you'll become some horrible terrible awful human being. Deep down we want to be good people, so if we're stuck between "get rich" and "be a good person" our subconscious opts in for being a good person. But here's the thing...

Money Makes You More Of Who You Already Are

Money allows you to be you on a bigger scale. If you're inherently a good person it enables you to do more amazing things, if you're inherently bad it allows you to do more crap. There are good poor people and bad poor people, just as there are good rich people and bad rich people; it's not the money, it's the person.

The media feeds us all of these negative sensational stories about these rich powerful corrupt people doing terrible stuff. Why? It sells! Scandals, big cover-ups, large companies doing bad things, etc. it's all they show us. Meanwhile, there's a greater amount of rich people doing amazing things like supporting charities, creating incredible legacies for humanity, and helping their fellow human being out.

If we all stopped watching the news until they started featuring the good and incredible positive stuff people do we'd all be better off. Which reminds me: STOP WATCHING THE NEWS. It's poison to the mindset you're trying to cultivate. For information that you absolutely need set an RSS feed to come to you or get the newspaper to read specific information you need (or, you know, just use the internet to look up latest news). I get it, there's certain information we need, for example, you might need to follow a company because you invested in their stocks, but most of the news featured feeds you negative garbage that you don't need.

The Information You Feed Your Mind Takes Root And Grows

When I was broke, and I mean ultra-broke, so broke that just to pay my rent and get basic groceries and toilet paper I had to go further into debt each month, I couldn't enjoy my free time. Not. One. Bit. Why? Because every damn minute I was stressing over how to make more money to get out of debt! Not to mention I couldn't afford to do anything I wanted, including invest in making films. Getting wealthy isn't about status or snobbery, it's about affording all of the things that enable you to T-H-R-I-V-E!

We Are Like Flowers Meant to Blossom Fully to Share Our Beauty with The World Before we Wither and Die

The truth is, life is alarmingly short. The time we have here on this earth is precious. Sitting at the end of our days in our death bed we want to be able to look back with no regrets, to be able to say, "I went for it! I did the stuff that scared the bejesus out of me, and you know what? It was awesome!"

Money gives you time, enables you to become the biggest most fully-grown flourishing version of you, and lets you glide through life with ease! Will there still be hard days and problems to deal with? Of course. But you'll be better equipped to deal with it all.

Money Is a Mindset

Becoming rich is all about changing the way you think about life. It isn't just about the money, but who you need to become to manifest it into your life! It is truly a growth process – so yes, expect some growing pains!

We are where we are in our lives because of our beliefs that fueled our past decisions. The habitual patterns our beliefs instilled in us created the result of where we are today. In order to grow, and have a different outcome in the future, we have to change those patterns and adopt new ones.

A New Vantage Point

One of the most important things we can do as we begin to reprogram our money beliefs is start assigning positive attributes to money. As long as money remains a 'negative' you'll subconsciously push it away, so now's the time to change that. We're going to start going through some positive money attributes, make note of the ones that make you feel especially good about money or that you find empowering:

- Money gives me more time to be with my loved ones
- Money lets me glide through life
- Money gives me all of the tools and resources I need to flourish
- Money gives me freedom of choice
- Money allows me to experience more aspects of life
- Money enables me to share my talents with the world
- Money lets me take care of my friends and family

Now write out 3 positive money statements the resonate with you.

Wealth Builder To-do List:

- Think about the negative money statements you have heard, picked up, or bought into, and realize that they aren't true – unless you believe in them! Choose to let them go.
- When faced with an either/or situation decide to choose both from now on!
- Write down your 3 positive money statements.
- Say out loud and proud: *Money gives me the means to fully flourish!*

CHAPTER 3: UNIVERSAL INTELLIGENCE

Before we go any further we need to talk about *Universal Intelligence*. This is the unseen force governing everything; the thing that goes beyond the physical, and the energy that makes up everything in the Universe. Call it whatever you want, God, Goddess, Spirit, Higher Power, Universe, Almighty, etc. the label doesn't matter. What matters is that there's a force, a power, a Universal Intellect, that has insight beyond our limited insight while we're in our physical bodies.

Now I used to get pretty grouchy and crotchety anytime anyone mentioned *God* (quite frankly I still picture this imaginary guy in a toga up in the clouds when I hear that word) but knowing there's something beyond our physical existence is important. This has nothing to do with religion or what happens after you die, but rather it has to do with how the Universe works and the Law of Attraction. If you want to get an upgrade in the financial department, this is an important component.

There are Forces Beyond What we can See Hard at Work Creating our Reality

The Law of Attraction

The crash course 101 on the Law of Attraction is this: Everything in the Universe is energy, both the physical and non-physical. All energy vibrates at varying frequencies. The Law of Attraction states that like attracts like. Your thoughts are energy, so when you focus on a thought, because like attracts like, you're attracting that thought into your physical reality.

In the Law of Attraction community, an often-used comparison is the Law of Gravity. You can't see it, but it's there. You don't live in fear that gravity won't be there for you and that you'll suddenly drift off into space, you trust that gravity is there doing its job and go about your day. The Law of Attraction is the exact same, you can't see it, but it's there, always working.

Now, before you object and say, "But we can prove gravity exists," let me step in and say you have proof of the Law of Attraction too. You have a lifetime of proof!

Everything that's come into your life was energetically attracted to you from your own mind.

Now before the bombardment of, "I don't think about how I want to be broke!" type statements get thrown about, give me a moment to explain. The context of your thought is irrelevant. Only the thought itself matters. What does that mean? That means that thinking, "I hate all of these damn bills!" is thinking about bills, and since you get more of what you think about, you attract more bills.

The Way that the Universe Responds to thought Is in the Most Simplistic Terms

Whatever the focus of your thought, that's what is reflected back to you. The context "want," or "don't want," is irrelevant. This may seem frustrating at first glance, but it makes this principle very easy to work with.

Focus Your Thoughts On the Things You Want to Attract

Now that you understand that context doesn't play a factor in the manifesting process, and that only what you focus on you attract more of, you can move forward with this. This is what it is to master your mindset, to use your thoughts with intention, and not dwell on the negatives. A focused mind can create results.

Our brains are incredible, they're super-computers that operate at incredible speeds. The amount of information they contain is staggering. Though just like running an online search, when you go to access information, your brain throws a whole lot of nonsense at you at the exact same time, all vying for your attention. Let me give you an example...

Search Input (Trying to remember or think of something): What was the name of my third-grade teacher?

Brain Output (thought stream): What did she even look like? Oh right, brown hair, glasses, pale skin... She droned on for hours about art... that school was drafty... why did they make us go outside at -30 for recess that one day? ... I'm hungry, I need to make lunch soon... I used to share my lunch with my third-grade best friend, I wonder what she's up to now?... Did Johnny Fitzsimmons have a crush on me too back then? What was I thinking about again? Oh, yup, third-grade teacher's name, hmmm... I should've asked mom to buy one of those yearbooks back then... Who am I kidding, when would I read it? I still haven't read that book on my nightstand... I need to pick up groceries later... Oh, right, it was Mrs. Reynolds.

It's simply not straight forward. There's a lot of random thoughts that come up as these off-shoots of the main theme. But there are ways to train your brain to become more focused, and also to deal with negative situations. You're human, you're going to stub your toe, and it's natural to be pissed off about it. What we want to avoid is dwelling on it, and instead move on from it and refocusing on what you do want again.

Mastering Your Mindset Begins with a Decision

Awareness is a choice. When you decide that, "From now on I'm going to be mindful of my thoughts," you've made that a commitment. While, like anything, it takes practice, if you decide that's who you are that's who you'll become.

Let's take a look at some ways to home-in your mind, and work on setting focus for your thoughts...

JOURNALING

If there's one helpful tool for getting our thoughts organized, it's writing them down. It forces us to slow down and give attention to the thoughts zooming around at light speed through our head. We can then examine them and become more aware of where our mind is dwelling.

This also gives you the opportunity to vent. We're human, and we have emotions, and repressing them or trying to pretend they don't exist just causes stress. Experience it and then let it go. Talking about a situation that has you upset, or writing about it, gets it out of your system so that you can move on.

Grab a journal and start writing in it in the mornings and/or evenings. Get your thoughts clear. Re-read what you write to see where your thoughts keep going and readjust when need be. Nothing brings more clarity than seeing exactly what you're thinking and feeling on paper.

ACCOUNTABILITY BUDDY

Is someone else in your life on the journey of personal growth? If yes, connect with them, and if not, make a new friend who is working on growing themselves too!

This person will be your accountability buddy, tell them about your own goals and plans, listen to theirs, and agree to touch base regularly to brainstorm and keep each other focused!

The journey to manifesting money is all about who you're becoming. The journey isn't a straight path, it's bumpy, so you need someone to tell you "It's OK, keep going!" every so often, just as much as to say, "You freakin' rock!" when you hit a milestone along the way.

Another human being can also see the things you're missing. In our lives, we only have a perspective from where we're at, what we know so far, and all of that is also limited by our beliefs. This means we often have opportunities dangling right in front of our faces that we're completely oblivious to. Working with another human being, sharing your ideas and aspirations, will inspire them with the many things that they can see available to you. Then when they share those possibilities you suddenly have the light-bulb moment and can move forward.

MEDITATION

Have you ever left your computer on without shutting it down for a really long time? Like days or weeks, or *cough* months? The longer it's on the more bogged down it gets, and the slower it processes new things, leaving you sitting waiting for a web page to load at snail speeds while you're screaming profanities and shaking your fist. That's what happens to your brain. Even when you're sleeping your brain is running your bodies vital processes while simultaneously processing dream imagery.

Your brain needs the opportunity to wind down and reboot. That's what meditating does for you. It lets your brain shut off all of the noise and reset, so it can then function more efficiently. It also gives you the opportunity to connect to your higher self (the part of you that's fully connected to Universal Intelligence so that you can get ideas and solutions to any problems you're currently experiencing).

Meditation is simple (in theory); you find a comfortable place to sit, close your eyes, let your mind rest, and focus on your breath. However, remember that it is called a *practice* for a reason; thoughts will bubble up throughout and we just need to gently release them as they do. Finding silence in our own head is ongoing work. Sometimes even getting to the silence prompts the thought, "Yay, I did it!" breaking the reverie and giving us a new thought to release.

The important thing is not to get angry or upset when the thoughts come. You're human and it's a natural part of this process. Simply recognize the thought, release it, and focus back in on your breath.

Even just a few minutes a day of dedicated silence to re-set your mind can change your life. As you continue to practice you will likely wish to add more time, however, know that any time is better than none. If some days you're busier than expected, even one minute will help you.

If you find the 'busy brain' chatter is really difficult for you to let go of, try playing some music, such as nature sounds, ocean waves, and other relaxation-based music to give your mind something to focus on. Some people also find it helpful to light a candle and to let their eyes focus on the flame as a way to clear the mind. Find what works for you and do that!

AFFIRMATIONS

We believe what we hear repeatedly. Since the person you hear the most from is yourself, your self-talk is imperative to defining your mindset. Affirmations are the predetermined beliefs you want to instill in your subconscious mind as your new truth.

The great thing about affirmations is you can whip them out at any time because you can say it in your head to yourself no matter what is going on around you. Your thoughts can be your greatest asset, it's all about being aware and reminding yourself of the life you're building and not getting 'stuck' in your current reality.

YOUR CURRENT REALITY

IS THE MANIFESTATION

OF YOUR PREVIOUS THOUGHTS

So, keep in mind that your current thoughts will define your future reality. What you see at present is just a reflection of the past. You have the ability to change the direction of your future at any given moment through your thoughts and beliefs.

You can make up your own affirmations, in fact, that's often best so they resonate with you and that you fully believe them. I'll share with you my favorite money mindset affirmations, if they resonate with you use 'em, and if not make up your own:

- I am a money magnet
- Money comes to me easily and effortlessly
- My current reality does not define me
- I am the master of my destiny
- I love money because money gives me the freedom to do what I want
- Nature is naturally abundant, and I am part of nature, so abundance abounds for me
- Money is all around me
- Money allows me to share my brilliance with the world
- I set my energetic frequency to vibe with money
- I am rich
- Money can't stay away from me
- I am ready and open to receiving money

Choose or create the affirmations you want to use, and then write them down and say them to yourself first thing in the morning, last thing before bed, and frequently during each day. This will get them stuck in your subconscious mind better than super glue! To instill new beliefs repetition is the key. We believe what we hear over and over again, that's how all of your current beliefs got in your mind, and that's how the new ones will stick too! Say them, think them, and most importantly *feel* into them!

GRATITUDE

If you were only to do 1 thing from this list of mighty mindset-building activities, I'd tell you do choose gratitude (although if you're serious about an upgrade in the financial department you'll commit to them all). Gratitude is the key to everything your heart desires; money, happiness, health, the dream job, relationships, vacations, having more time to enjoy the things you love, and everything else you could ever want in life. Gratitude focuses your thoughts on the things and experiences you want, and supercharges them with emotion, making you a magnetic beacon to attract those things to yourself.

The great thing about emotions is that you can't feel 2 opposing emotions at the same time. This is why gratitude is so amazing. When you're grateful, you're not sad, angry, hateful, upset, or sad; gratitude shifts you into positive emotions. To be grateful we have to consciously be thankful for a situation, person, or thing, and since we get more of what we focus on, gratitude ensures you're attracting more of what you want into your life.

You can implement gratitude in two ways:

Grateful for What I Have

Being grateful for what you already have is incredibly important. If you don't appreciate what you already have, you won't be getting anything more. Remember:

WHAT YOU APPRECIATE APPRECIATES

No matter your current situation, there are many things to be grateful for. You're reading this book, which means you're alive for one. It also means you had the money to get this book or got it gifted to you, or leant, all meaning you attracted it into your life. You are a manifesting magnet! One of the best things you can implement is making a list every day, either in your head or on paper, of 10 things you're grateful for!

In terms of being grateful for money specifically, it's important to remember that money isn't just what's in your bank account or wallet. It's what it's bought for you over the course of your entire life. None of us get a free ride, money is there to make it all happen...

As a child, money is paid for you. Did you have food to eat? A roof over your head? After school activities? Toys? Books? New clothes as you grew? A bike? A bed? Textbooks, pencils, pens, and notebooks for school? Field trips? Medical care? A college fund?

As an adult, we get an innumerable amount of things that we wouldn't have without money. Did you get post-secondary schooling & live in a dorm? Have a car, bike, or public transit? Food? Heat? A comfy seat? Electricity? An apartment or house to live in? Gas? Furniture? Computer? Phone? Television? The list goes on and on.

Money provides us with all of the conveniences of life! It also enables us to shine, to bring our best self forward, to learn, grow, and explore this planet in so many incredible ways. Money is the conduit to both material things and experiences, so when we're grateful for anything in our life (time with family, our home, a great vacation, etc.) it's money that enables us to have more of those incredible experiences and things. That's why being grateful for everything and anything, not just specifically money itself, makes you a money magnet!

Here are some categories to inspire you when you're making your daily list of 10 things to be grateful for:

- Love
- Health
- Relationships
- Family
- Friends
- Work
- Career
- Time
- Travel
- Pets
- Food & Water
- Nature
- Home & Hearth
- Art
- Entertainment
- Anything You Think Of

Grateful for What I Want

The second way we can use gratitude is for things and experiences we want to attract into our lives. Thinking about, and being grateful for, something we don't yet have is the surest way for it to show up in our lives. If it's on your mind it will soon be in your life. Not only will your thoughts begin attracting it to you, but what we focus on we move towards as well; we're basically walking-talking energetic magnets.

What you Seek Seeks You

One of the best ways to put this into practice is through *visualization*. Visualization lets you go through the experience of receiving that desire in your mind, making it feel more real. The more detail in your visualization, the better.

So, the first step, decide on what it is you want. Get clear on what you'd like to manifest into your life. Once you have that, find a quiet place to sit, get comfortable, close your eyes and imagine receiving the news that you just got the thing you want to manifest. Work through the visualization by imagining answers to the following unfolding before you:

- Where are you?
- Who tells you the news?
- How does it make you feel?
- What can you see, hear, smell, taste, and touch?
- Who is the first person you tell?
- How do you celebrate?

By getting in depth into your visualization you get into the specifics, and the Universe loves specifics. The clearer a picture you have of what you want, the better the Universe can deliver. It also makes it more real for you, bolstering your belief and faith that it is coming to you!

Wealth Builder To-do List:

- Commit to starting 3 of the activities above to start honing your awareness today and to start the rest by the end of the week. *Making these activities the first thing you do when you wake up can profoundly change your life; they set up your day to start with positivity and intention
- When life feels stressful or overwhelming remind yourself that you are part of something much bigger, that you and everything else in the Universe is energy, and that by shifting your thoughts at any given moment you are changing your future
- Say out loud and proud: *Money is energy, and I am energy, we are one!*

CHAPTER 4: WHAT IS MONEY?

We talked a tiny bit about what money actually *is* earlier, a means to an end, but it's important we dig a bit deeper into this. Money has been painted as this big bad wolf by society, and as long as it remains that way in our heads, we ain't gonna be attracting much of it. So, let's really, truly, once and for all, get clear about what money is.

Money is...

- By dictionary definition: *A circulating medium of exchange*
- A glorified I.O.U.
- A value assigned coin, paper, or often nowadays digital number, given a value that can then be exchanged for goods or services

As you can plainly see, money is quite simply a tool for exchange. Plain and simple.

Money is NOT...

- Evil
- Vindictive
- Hateful
- Spiteful

- Elusive
- Avoiding you

These negative emotional assignments that we give to money are our own hang-ups. Money never walked up to you on the street and slapped you for no reason, did it? I mean seriously, money is just minding its own business, trying to live its life, and we're over here bad mouthing it like gossipy school girls. We need to break free of those old patterns and accept money for what is really is.

Money is Energy

Everything at its base form is energy, including money. You will attract or repel it based on your own energetic frequency. If you are constantly thinking and saying how awful money is, it's not going to come to hang out with you.

Personification

A really helpful exercise is to personify money. Pretend money is a friend of yours. Now, imagine money heard all of the stuff you've said and thought about him over the years. Would money be sticking around or unfriending you and telling you to never call, text, or show up at his place ever again? It's food for thought.

One of the easiest ways to get those thoughts and feelings straight is to write a letter to your friend money. Tell money in this letter how you feel about him – all of it. Leave nothing out. See what comes up. This is one of my old letters to money:

Dear Money,

I'm so utterly frustrated by you. You're never here when I need you. And as soon as you show up you leave. I never have enough of you.

I hate that I'm in debt because I don't make enough of you. I'm stressed out and I can't sleep, and I resent you for it. Why can't you just be here?

I'm disgusted by what people do for you. I think you make people waste their time on this earth chasing after you. I'm not willing to waste my life chasing after you.

Can you please just freaking show up and stay so I can move on with my life?

As you can see all I did was tell money how much I disliked it. It's no wonder it never came by! I certainly wouldn't show up for someone who wrote that kind of letter to me.

Money's Many Forms

When we discuss money in terms of manifesting, it can arrive in for us in various forms. Money can show up as:

- Money (Paper, coin, check, digits in your bank account)
- A discount
- Someone lending or gifting you something you were going to purchase thereby saving you money
- A coupon
- A sale
- A rebate
- A refund
- A normally paid service you get for free

As you can see it's not just showing up as currency. When we view all of the many ways that money shows up we can see it's there for us more often than we realized.

Money is a Blank Slate

The most important thing for you to remember is that money has the meaning you give it. It's a blank slate to represent what you want it to represent. Because money unlocks the doors for you to be, do, and have whatever your heart desires, it's meaning is limitless.

This is why focusing on money itself makes it hard to manifest. Money itself is just paper and coins. Sure, it's exciting to watch the amount in our banks account climb, but that excitement wears off quickly. What is the money for? Focus on that and you'll attract the money that enables you to do and have what you want.

Wealth Builder To-do List:

- Write a letter to money to tell it how you feel, then re-read your letter and see what fears, doubts, and blocks you're harboring around money.
- Think through this past week. What were all of the ways that money came to you? Write them down, then say "Thank you, thank you, thank you for <u>(However money came to you)</u>. I am surrounded by abundance!" for each one.
- Say out loud and proud: *Money is a blank slate that I give meaning to!*

CHAPTER 5: MONEY MINDSET

Manifesting money into your life starts and ends with your mindset. It isn't just about the money; it's about who you need to be to have it. If your financial situation isn't where you want it to be, chances are there's some personal growth necessary for you to do first. The Universe only gives us what we can handle.

Did you know that 70% of lottery winners and people who come into a large windfall of money will go broke and declare bankruptcy within 3-5 years? It's not even that the majority go and spend recklessly, but their money mindset was set for a much lower amount, and suddenly they have all of this money and it feels like a bottomless pit that will never run out. But it's not.

Most people take the approach of, "Once I have money I'll learn how to manage it." That is a backward way of thinking. Remember, energy flows where your attention goes, so by focusing on money, and learning how to handle it *before* you have it means you'll then get it. You need to set your mindset to wealthy before the money comes to you, in order for you to attract it, keep it, and make it grow.

We'll discuss how to make and handle money in the coming chapters, but for now, we will focus on your mindset. This is the very first thing that needs to change in order for your bank account to change. Your mind governs your financial reality.

Your Mindset Is Your Moneymaker

The only thing standing between us and the financial reality we desire is us. Our thoughts dictate our reality. Think of your thoughts like a preview of what's to come; just like watching television, if you don't like what you see you need to change the channel.

LEARN FROM SUCCESSFUL WEALTHY PEOPLE

I'm not sure why we make things so hard on ourselves. There is no need to recreate the wheel when it comes to building wealth, it's been done over and over again. Many, many, people have already done it, and all that we need to do in order to get there ourselves is to follow in their footsteps.

If we take the time to step back and observe how a wealthy person thinks and acts, we can then emulate that for our own success. So, what do wealthy people do & think to be successful?

Wealthy People Know Their Numbers

It's underrated, but knowing your numbers is a big part of wealth building, and wealthy people know this. It can seem a daunting task at first, and if you're in debt with a barren bank account it can make you feel inclined to stick your head in the sand and pretend to not see what's happening rather than want to take the time to delve into it. But the first step in changing your financial reality is to get very clear on what's happening around money in your life. Best of all, if you're thinking about money, you'll be attracting more to you.

This doesn't have to take long and isn't as complicated as you may think. You can, if you wish, see a financial planner at your banking institution, or contact one of the incredible ladies from the directory at the back of the book, who may have some suggestions based on your spending habits. These consultations are usually free.

What you need to do is understand where you're at before you can make changes. Go through and understand all of your income & expenses to get a better understanding of your financial situation.

Grab a piece of paper and a pen and get your numbers on a *monthly* basis for the following sources of income and expenses (don't guess, look the accurate numbers up):

Income

Working Income:

Your working income would be defined as the income you are putting in time to generate, most commonly this is your job. It could be earned hourly, by salary, or through commissions. If your income changes month to month add up your total earnings from the past 3 months and divide the total by 3 to get the average monthly income to use as your baseline.

Passive income:

Passive income streams would be any monies coming to you that you are not having to actively work for (anymore). Most passive income streams take a good effort to set up in the beginning, and then the payments continue to come in there-after. Some examples are from royalties, ongoing customer repeat orders, dividends, etc. (we will later discuss how to get passive income streams set up).

Investments:

Property, stocks, art, gold, etc. – anything you own that's of value, and best of all appreciates in value, is an investment. It's good to take account of what you've put money into that could be liquidated for cash.

Debt:

Anything you owe falls under debt. This can be what's left on your mortgage, a loan, what's left to pay off on your car, student loans, credit card debt, the money you owe a friend, etc. Anything you owe is a debt. Write it all down and add it all up so this is no longer an ambiguous number.

Expenses:

Expenses will be the monthly payments we make for necessities & enjoyment:

- Mortgage/Rent
- Utilities (hydro, gas, & water)

- Internet
- Phone
- Insurance (if you pay quarterly or yearly for insurance break that down into what it would be monthly)
- Groceries (food as well as to include paper products, cleaning products, and grooming products)
- Medicine
- Property Tax
- Clothing
- Entertainment
- Anything else that's a regular monthly purchase or bill

Wealthy People Manage Their Money

Getting money is one thing, and managing its allocation is another. Rich people understand their financial situation and work to improve upon is by eliminating debt, increasing investments and net worth, and finding new ways to generate passive income. They understand the balance needed, and also play the long game. A wealth mindset focuses on the goal, *financial freedom*, over immediate gratification.

Financial freedom is going to look different for everyone. Essentially, it means having the wealth to live a desired lifestyle. If you need the mansion, sports cars, and diamonds, to be fulfilled then that would be the depiction of financial freedom for you – but that's not the only definition. Living with the means to pay for whatever it is you need to shine bright and thrive is what financial freedom is all about. That means the amount of money needed varies greatly from person to person. Get clear on your ideal lifestyle, do the numbers, and figure out what you'd need to make it a reality.

Once you know where you're at and what you're working toward you can begin to take action. It's easier to say 'no' to that sale item you really want when you know putting that money into an investment gets you closer to your overall goal. Now, this isn't about depriving yourself along the way either, you need to enjoy life too, but it becomes a balance in both regards. Cutting out 'shopping therapy' is just as important as allowing yourself something fun along the road. Balance is the key here.

Wealthy People Play to Win

What happens in any sports game if the team ONLY plays on the defense? At best it's a stalemate. You cannot win if you play defense only, you have to go all in for the win.

When it comes to the money game the majority of people don't play to win, they play not to lose. This mindset will never amount to creating abundance. Its fear based and perpetuates a deep seeded belief that there's not enough and if you lost what you had that you could never get it back.

Money doesn't work like that. Money is cyclical, I mean it, it literally circulates. When we pay for goods or services the money doesn't just go *Poof!* and disappear, it cycles to someone else. The same happens when you earn money. It's constantly exchanging hands. On top of that money isn't finite, they just keep printing more of it every single day. It's not a diminishing resource, it's an ever-growing one.

Playing to win means believing in yourself and making the no-nonsense decision to do whatever it takes (besides cheating, illegal, or immoral stuff) to make it happen. This is the attitude of winners. Decide to play on the offensive.

Wealthy People Have Good Money Habits

It is our habits that define our lives and that make up the majority of what we do on any given day, and it is from those habits that we create our results. Habits often seem insignificant, but over time they add up in a big way. Habits aren't just about biting your nails when you're stressed out, they encompass all of our automatic actions. Success begins with habits in all areas of life; exercising and eating well is a habit, being good with money is a habit, being effective with time is a habit.

Wealthy people know the power of habit and consciously have built habits that support wealth building. The excellent thing with habits is that we can easily to adapt to them. Within a few days of repeating an action we come to expect it, and after 21 days it's an engrained activity.

Wealthy People Have a Morning Routine

If you've read or listen to interviews with successful people, you'll see very distinctively that almost all will discuss the importance of their morning routine. Your thoughts and actions at the very beginning of the day determine your entire success (or lack thereof) for the rest of the day.

Think of a day you woke up in a bad mood. Maybe you had a bad dream or stubbed your toe getting out of bed, and it left you feeling agitated. This negative attitude left unchanged can then follow you around all day attracting more things to be grumpy about. Like-attracts-like and therefore a seemingly minor thing spirals into a really bad day.

Successful people take the reins and don't allow that to happen. No matter the mood they wake up in, they take the time to consciously shift their thoughts, and do some proactive activities that set them up to be more focused and energized to tackle their day. In a later chapter, we will discuss how to craft your own morning routine for success.

Wealthy People Focus on Personal Development

Self-improvement is a never-ending journey. This is something that wealthy and successful people understand. Improving oneself on an ongoing basis is the key to continual growth and continued success. This can be in the form of a mentor, coach, reading, audiobooks, seminars, webinars, thinktanks, and just about anything else that forces them to grow and learn. The number one thing to remember on your path to riches is this: it's not about what you're trying to gain, it's about who you're becoming, that attracts wealth.

Wealthy People Set Goals

Almost everyone has a dream, something they want to do, see, or be, but rarely does it pass this wishful-wanting stage. A dream only becomes a goal when we make the no-nonsense decision to go for it with all we've got. Setting goals are one of the most critical pieces of the puzzle, and successful people understand this. If you don't know where you're going in life, then you aren't going anywhere. Picking a goal and setting a deadline to achieve it forces us into action in order to achieve it. Remember: if it ain't got a deadline then it's just a dream.

Wealthy People Take Action

Action is the bridge between the non-physical and physical worlds. It is what brings thought energy into the physical realm. Successful people understand that once they have their goal they have to get themselves into action, any action, and to watch for cues from the Universe for the next steps. You cannot know everything before beginning, course correcting is a part of the process, so don't wait, act.

Wealthy People Take Risks

This doesn't mean taking foolish risks, but it is about learning what you can as quickly as you can, making an assessment, and then either getting in the game or finding another opportunity. You've heard the saying, "The bigger the risk the greater the reward," and the adage holds true. The key is not just taking a gamble and hoping for the best but getting fully involved to see it through to fruition. This comes from the successful person's belief in themselves and their ability to make decisions and see them through.

Wealthy People Believe in Themselves

Successful people believe in themselves and their own ability to take charge and do what's necessary to succeed. It's the person, not the opportunity, that determines success. They are also used to flexing their faith muscle in knowing the Universe has their back. When they take on a project they don't just hope it works, they know it will work because they will make it work.

Wealthy People Make Decisions

Ambiguity and indecision are the death of opportunity. Successful people decide what they want and then take definitive action towards making it happen. They know that when they make choices they can accomplish one thing and then move onto another.

What trips up the majority of people in making a decision is feeling that either, 1. They'll be missing out on all of the other possibilities, or 2. They'll make the wrong choice, and nothing will pan out. By not choosing they don't get to do anything, so they miss out on everything. And by not trying, they're failing without even giving it a chance.

Make a decision, go for it, see it through, and then you can try something new once you're done. It's winning all around and will bring many victories and new experiences. Once the decision is made you've given yourself permission to go all in and flourish.

Wealth Builder To-do List:

- Pick a successful wealthy person and read up on them to discover what their path to success was
- Know your numbers! Go through the activity in discovering where your finances are at
- Say out loud and proud: *I choose to think and act like the wealthy do to build my own riches!*

CHAPTER 6: MAKING MONEY

My dad is a small business owner, an entrepreneur, who always toted the motto, "Work smarter not harder." These are words to live by and I suggest that you write them down and put them up somewhere you'll see them daily. Think about it, if people only got paid by how hard they worked rich people would be run into the ground instead of luxuriating in more time off to spend doing things they love.

WORK SMARTER NOT HARDER

There's no "one right way" to success and financial freedom, after all, we each have our own individual goals and desires. However, there are some important principles that everyone should apply. These are the principles that will get your income booming, no matter what it's coming in from.

Do What You Love & The Money Will Come

Quite frankly this is the most important thing for you to remember. There's this major misconception, the belief that you can either do something you love (and be broke) or make money (doing something you don't care for). This is the biggest pile of bull dung out there. Studies have been done proving otherwise; if you pursue what you love, you're more passionate, more determined to make it succeed, and often have more opportunities to profit from it.

Turn your passion into profit. Just because you love it and find it easy to do, doesn't mean that's the case for everyone. For some reason when something comes easily to us we devalue it and assume it's a simple task for all. That's simply not the case, we each have our own unique talents and gifts that, from someone else's perspective, are totally awe-inspiring. Stand in your power, shine that talent, and charge people for it!

Income Streams

We discussed Income, Passive Income, and Investments briefly in Chapter 5, and now we're going to dive into how to set them up to generate money for you.

Working Income

Working income is the type of earnings that the majority of people are used to and understand. This tends to come from an employer, or, if you're a small business owner, it is the wage you pay out to yourself. This pay is commonly in the form of salary, hourly wage, or commission payouts (or a combination thereof).

This type of income rarely offers the opportunity for financial freedom by itself, as it is dependent on the continual effort and time of each individual. It also often caps income your potential (unless you work commission based). When your income is capped or dependent solely on the amount of time you can put in then you don't have enough hours in your life to exchange for financial freedom.

Exchanging Time for Money Limits the Amount You Can Make

Working income is often a necessary upfront task for almost everyone. It covers the necessities and gives you money to then grow into more money. The problem is most people don't know how to go beyond working income to generate monetary streams that trickle into their account even while they sleep.

We've been so programmed as a society in western culture to go to school, get a good education, and get a good job. The end. But that's not the end. In fact, we know there's an issue with this model now because we have more people qualified (and often overqualified) for the same job than can be hired for it. And even if you are the person that gets hired, then what? You have a capped wage that prevents you from getting ahead, and the company raises usually barely keep up with the cost of inflation.

This is why relying on working income alone is not the path to riches. Perhaps you have a job or career you absolutely love and there's nothing else you'd want to do, there's nothing wrong with that. However, if your income has a ceiling, then in order to become wealthy, you need additional revenue streams. This is where creating passive income and investing comes into play.

Passive Income

Passive income comes in many forms and allows you to free up your time and earn money while you're doing... whatever you want! This is the kind of income everyone dreams about, but very few people seem to understand how to do it. It's kind of like the mystical unicorn of income that people aren't really sure exists, or if they do believe in it, they've never seen it.

So first off, it does exist, and I'm happy to inform you

that it's not all that complicated to get it set up. You create whatever it is you need to create that will thereafter be able to run mostly on auto-pilot while you watch the money trickle into your bank account. The catch is, you generally have a significant amount of upfront work to do before you see even 1 cent of income. This scares off most people, but it shouldn't. What if I told you that if you put in 1 year of dedicated unpaid hard work that I'd pay you every year for the rest of your life? 1 year of work = many years' worth of income = yes, please!

This is how it works. Now, the time it takes you to set up your passive income could vary wildly, it could take you 1 month or 5 years depending on what it is, and also depending on what you choose to do you might earn some profits along the set-up part of the journey. Let's take a look at some tried and true passive income streams that you can set up:

Write a Book

I don't care who you are, you've got something book-worthy to share. The human experience teaches us each something unique, and we can share that to help each other grow. Maybe you naturally love to make up stories, but even if you don't, storytelling is intrinsic to our nature. Every time we talk, tell someone about our day, or something that happened, we're telling a story.

A book, no doubt, is an upfront effort to write and prepare, however, it's not as monumental a task as most think. Like anything, tackling it bit by bit it will get done. This boils down to habits and consistency. The benefit of all of that upfront hard work is once your book is completed and, on the market, it's a source of residual royalty payments for as long as you make it available for sale!

If you're an entrepreneur, business professional, coach, small business owner, professional speaker, or in any line of work that serves clients and customers, writing a book is an excellent way to drum up new business. As a published author you become an authority on your topic. Your book sales will drive new customers and clients to you, and your current clients will want to buy your book, so it's a doubly effective strategy.

One of the things that held me back from getting published was having no clue about the publication process or marketing of books. Once I did my research and had a rock-solid understanding of what to do, and how to make sure my books sold, it was easy to move forward. I've put together a 3-week online course to help others who feel land-locked in the "How do it I it?" of it all, to guide you through how to write, publish, and market your book successfully:

https://www.udemy.com/get-published-workshop/

Or grab a copy of my book:

Get Published Workbook: Write | Publish | Market

Music

Since the music world has turned from CDs to digital downloads it's opened up the door for many new musicians to enter the scene. So, if this is you, get your songs written and practiced, rent a recording studio, jam out, and put those babies up for sale. There are so many platforms online to do it with, take your pick. Then, once the work is up, put on your marketing hat and get to work (we'll discuss more about marketing later).

Social Media Influencer

Before you roll your eyes and say, "Yeah sure, me, a social media influencer... right, I'll go do that with my whopping 100 followers..." remember that all of these things are, 1. Learnable, 2. Take a little while to set up, 3. Doable.

If you already had a 100K people following you on social you'd already be doing it, I get it. But it's not impossible to build a following, it's not magic, and it's not just for movie stars. There is a tactical way to build a following on any platform, and it comes down to learning the platform, picking a niche, using the appropriate way to build a following (for example on Instagram the photos better be popping), making yourself easy to find, and interacting. Social media is a skill, so set out to learn it. Even if you don't plan to be an influencer you need it for marketing anything else you choose to pursue.

There is a ton of information via blogs, books, YouTube videos, online courses, etc. that can help you learn the skills to build a following. Gary Vaynerchuk and Chalene Johnson are 2 social media guru's I highly recommend following and learning from.

Once you have the following, and even when it's building up, you'll be able to:

1. Offer services as an Influencer (people will pay for this service and/or offer free product)
2. Have people coming to you to represent their brand/product
3. Have an audience to share your product/service to

Affiliate Marketing

We recommend products all of the time, so why in the world not get paid for it? Almost every major and minor site offers affiliate marking nowadays, making it easier than ever to get some extra money floating into your account for doing something you were already going to do. You can also step it up a notch by using affiliate links on your own website and social media platforms.

Think about what products (or the stores the products are sold at) that you recommend to people regularly already. Make a list and then go to those websites and see which ones offer you the ability to become an affiliate and then sign up!

An added bonus is a lot of these other passive income streams can be intertwined. For example, let's say you write a book and then it sells on Amazon and you are an Amazon affiliate. When you give out your book link for people to buy it, you give it using your affiliate link, therefore getting your book royalty AND affiliate payout all from one purchase.

Network Marketing

I cannot speak highly enough about Network Marketing and the benefits it carries with it. Network Marketing gives you a ready-made business. It's basically the equivalent of getting a franchise, but without the hefty and often $100,000+ investment of a brick and mortar store. The products are there, ready for drop shipping from the company warehouses, so you don't have to have product on hand, or ship, or take returns, or pay overhead; it's all taken care of for you. All you need to do is build a customer base and a team.

This is a business model based solely on making and building relationships. Is it sales? Yes, but so is everything else in life. Trying to get your kid to eat their veggies? You're selling them on veggies. Trying to convince your spouse to see the movie that you want to see at the theatre? You're selling them on the movie. Sales are an everyday thing, it is not about being a pushy-gross-overbearing-jerk, but instead about helping someone solve a problem with your product.

There is an incredible amount of benefits from having a Network Marketing Business. First of all, as a home business, there are some great tax incentives. Second, it's easy to learn, and anyone can do it. Third, you end up having this awesome tribe of people around you who have the same interests – you'll build friendships you never expected! Repeat business is big in these companies, so once you have a loyal customer you'll find residual income flows in. Fourth, these companies give you free marketing training! So instead of having to invest in learning these skills, you'll learn while you earn.

The main income in network marketing comes from team building. When you build a team, the reps you get into your downline then generate the majority of your income (it's not taken from their income but rather an incentive from the company paid to you for helping them learn). This means it's beneficial for you to take the time to build a team and help those people become successful – everyone wins!

Want to work and learn from me? Come join my team:

www.AmandaRoseFitness.com

Blog

Blogging is such an incredible tool for passive income. In the age of the internet, we are addicted to blogs. If a title piques our interest, we can't help but click the link to read the full article. Within the article, it's simple to incorporate related purchase suggestions, discuss a related product or service, or get readers to sign up for a mailing list. This incorporates selling your product/service and/or affiliate marketing integration.

Online Courses

I love online course creation. Anything you could teach in person you can now teach online. It's easier than ever because you can simply create your course content, get it on a platform, and after that, all you need to do is market it to bring in students and have the money roll in.

You can teach just about anything. Knitting, jewelry making, marketing, the finer art of table setting, how to bake the perfect cake, pottery making, growing the perfect tulip, how to get a date; if you know how to do it someone else wants to learn it. Video, text, slides; the way to convey information is versatile and lets you have creativity in the way you present it.

You can run courses through e-mail, in a Facebook group, through a click-funnel, using a pre-existing online platform for course building, or by creating your own web platform. The sky is the limit, and it's a fun and easy way to create passive income streams.

Online Shop

I am over the moon about how integrated everything is now. There are some seriously kick-butt e-commerce platforms out there that can simplify your life; basically, set it up and let 'er go! My dear friend Jennifer Verardi has put this into practice with her clothing line for her yogi business *Tree Star* (www.TreeStar.ca).

With the simplicity of web integration, Jennifer's main work came up front for her clothing line: designing the graphics and text. Next, she ordered some samples to make sure they looked right, made a few adjustments, got in a second order, approved the designs, and then got them up on her website for order. Now when customers order the apparel they go through her checkout, my friend gets paid, and the order is sent off to the manufacturer to be printed and shipped to the customer, easy-peasy.

Is there work in marketing to get people to find her website? Absolutely. But the time involved in marketing isn't overly intensive, and the time-consuming aspect (product creation) is handled elsewhere.

This can be done with many types of items where manufacturing and shipping are handled elsewhere with drop shipping, and you simply integrate it through your e-commerce platform. It also takes minimal time to set up, making it one of the easiest options to get money rolling in passively faster. Go online and explore some e-commerce platforms, or if you want to create your own website and find your own manufacturer that's an option too!

Use Your Imagination

Got your own idea for a passive income stream? Go for it! The ones above are tried and true and give you a firm idea of what's available to you, and what's involved. You can do as many as you want and rock those income streams, so your bank account keeps on bumping up with deposits!

Wealth Builder To-do List:

- Understand and accept that working income is only a part of the equation and don't rely on it solely to become financially free
- Pick a passive income option and get the ball rolling with it so that you set yourself up for ongoing passive income streams
- Say out loud and proud: *I welcome all income streams! I make money even while I'm asleep!*

CHAPTER 7: MARKETING

Whatever you're choosing to do to make extra income, or get a business up off the ground, marketing is the key. It doesn't matter if you've got the best product or service on the entire planet, if no one knows about it then it won't sell. Knowing what resonates with buyers is the key to good marketing.

With the digital age, marketing can be done in a very inexpensive way. No longer do you need to buy a TV spot for a commercial, or save up for a billboard, or a page in a magazine. Of course, you could add in those elements, but online you can reach the whole world.

DIGGIN' THE PERSONAL TOUCH

After years of getting over inundated by big businesses, and then inevitably dealing with the challenges of not-so-personal customer service, small businesses are making a massive come back. People want to buy from someone who will take the time to address their needs and be there for them if they have a problem. Big in-your-face ads don't work anymore, people want to make a connection: enter the *Entrepreneur*.

A Win for the Little Guy

Entrepreneurship and small businesses are now dominating the playing field in business. Do not get me wrong, I have NOTHING against big businesses. They employ a ton of people and help drive down costs with their capacity for mass production, I love big businesses. What I am saying is that now you don't *have* to be a big company to do substantial business or get clients.

This has changed the climate in which we market our products and services. Traditional advertising is all but dead, with a pulse that's continually fading.

MARKETING

Sales are the lifeblood of any company. No sales and the company will fold, fast. It is the most crucial aspect of any business. Marketing is how you'll reach your buyer and make the sale. Mastering marketing in all of its many forms would be a several book endeavor so we're going to focus on some of the crucial elements and tactics to reach people.

The Goal Isn't to Sell

The Goal is to Help People

If you try to sell, you won't. Selling in a push-it-on-someone way is icky, for you and for them. But setting out with an intention to help someone, that feels good for everyone and actually closes the sale. Remember the power of intention every time you set out to sell or market. Always ask yourself, "How can I serve them?"

Target Market

The most important thing you need to decide upfront is who you're trying to talk to. I hear all too often, "Well, I think my product is something everyone would enjoy." I'm sorry to say that won't cut it.

IF YOUR TRY TO TALK TO EVERYONE

YOU END UP TALKING TO NO ONE

There's a fear that homing in on an audience will negate business from other people who don't fit into that mold. A lot of amateur marketing campaigns go so broad, trying to be for everyone, that their message hits home with no one, and ultimately tanks. In reality, people are unique, we all like different things, and if the right target ad lands in front of us we can't whip out our credit card fast enough to get it.

The more specific you can get the better. Understand who your buyer is, what their interests are, and what problem they need to have solved. The best thing you can do is put yourself in your buyer's shoes. There's a high chance whatever you're selling you personally use, but in the rare case that's not so, then it's crucial to put the shoe on the other foot and imagine being the buyer. If you do use it and you are the ideal customer archetype then start to make a list of your wants, needs, interests, and demographics.

If I know that I'm marketing to married women age 35-40, who love knitting, jogging, and are stay-at-home moms on a tight budget, the ad is going to look a lot different than if I was marketing an ad to 25-30-year-old women who are single, career driven, yoga class enthusiasts, with a hefty savings account. They have different wants, needs, and problems to be solved. If you know who you're talking to then you can talk to them in a way that resonates.

Keywords

Once you have your target market depicted, then you can move into a deeper understanding of how to reach them. You know who this person is, and their wants and needs, so what are they searching for? There's a reason metadata is highly sought after and well paid for; companies want to know what people are looking for, so that they can send targeted ads.

While yes, you could opt to pay for this information, you can also take some time to get to know your ideal client by doing some creative thinking. This can be helpful to do with other people as you can discuss the process. Basically, we're taking a little dive into psychology for behavior, but you don't need a degree in psychology to do this.

Let's do a little example...

Let's say you've created the world's BEST cheese slicer! I mean this thing is freaking awesome; it's got 10 different ways to angle it for cheese slice thickness, the top corner has a sharp edge for seamlessly cutting cheese squares, it's lightweight, yet durable, and it's aesthetically beautiful so it can be left on the cheese plate for guests to use. It's everything a cheese connoisseur could have ever wanted! On top of that, it's well priced so the everyday use factor is there too. You know that cheese lovers need this in their kitchen!

You've gone through the process of finding your target market, and have determined that men age 35-50, who work in the business sector, are married, and enjoy cooking, dinner parties, & watching HGTV, are your ideal customer. The next step is determining what this ideal customer browses for online. If you can nail down the keywords that will ensure your ad pops up in front of your ideal customer, then *bam*, you are connecting your product to your buyer!

The novice mistake with keywords is assuming the customer is searching for your product. Most of the time, they won't be. Think of the way you search online, it's often not to specifically buy something (sometimes it is, but most commonly not), but to look up information on the things we're interested in. While, yes, you want to include keywords such as "cheese slicer" "Kitchen utensil" etc. you do not want to limit them to these types.

So, with your archetype above what kinds of things would this person search for? Let's brainstorm some possibilities:

- Info about favorite HGTV shows and their hosts
- Suits, ties, and dress clothes
- Fine wines

- Vacations and couples' retreats
- Hardware stores for home renovation
- Gardening supplies and shops
- Beard grooming
- Recipes

As you can see just from this short list you have 100s of keywords you could use as offshoots – names of TV shows and hosts, clothing brands, shoe brands, names of stores they'd search regularly, etc. The key takeaway here is with some powers of deduction and putting yourself in your ideal customer's shoes, you can determine how to reach them with your ad.

Social Media Marketing

Social media has given us this incredible ability of connectivity. No matter the platform, we can now connect with other people in a whole new and unique way. If you're someone who dislikes social media, I'm telling you now, it's time to change that mindset.

I used to hate the idea of social media. It seemed like this giant time-suck, and when I first got sucked onto it all it seemed like to me was like a place for people to brag, show off, bitch & complain, or tear each other down. It didn't occur to me at the time that it was simply the circle of people surrounding me at the time. I often see people complain of those insights now - and if that's you, it is *not* social media you dislike, it's the people you are friends with/following on those platforms that are driving you mad.

Figure out the True Source Of Negativity Then Get Rid of It

When your news feed is full of awesome stuff from really incredibly positive, uplifting, motivational people, it's a dream to be on there! Sure, we all have bad days, but when it's complaint after complaint day after day that's when I draw the line. If a person can't learn and grow from what's happening in their life they're doomed to repeat it, and that's when we see those complainers hard at work on our social feeds.

So, before you market on social media, you will want your social media to be a positive place to spend time on, which means a social media clean up:

- Delete/Block/Unfollow toxic people on your list

- Decide that social media is a positive place for growth and sharing; your mindset determines the outcome of everything in your life so set your belief to attract awesome things and people!
- Follow inspirational, motivational, kickass people who inspire you
- Make the commitment to contribute content that lifts other people up, inspires them, and serves them

Now as far as marketing on social media, that's an ever-changing ball-game. There are constant and fast-paced changes that occur in the social media game as these platforms change their algorithm's and audiences change with the times. For that reason, I'm not going to go over specifically what's working right now, because a year from now that will have changed, and whenever it changes we can all go to the amazing social media guru's who will share the changes and how to adapt on their blog/channel for us to update ourselves with. What I will tell you are the timeless basics that will be steadfast over the years.

- **Give a lot, ask a little.** It doesn't matter how big or small you are, or how big or small your following is, you need to give more to your audience than you ask from them in return. Why should I follow you? Because your content is valuable to me. There are millions of people on every platform I can pick from to follow, so I'm going to follow the ones that give me value. Value can be information, inspiration, motivation, wisdom, DIY hacks, etc. anything that is of value to the people seeing it. That doesn't mean it has to be long and complicated, it just needs to be worth the viewers time to read/watch. Then, occasionally, when you throw out an 'ask' (which would be an offer, a product or service to buy, a course to sign up for, etc.) you've proven that you deliver value, and your audience trusts you enough to take you up on buying whatever you're selling.

- **Be Yourself.** Comparison is the death of happiness and trying to be someone you're not will end in misery. I know, that's hard. There are people we see on social media who are knocking it out of the park and it's like "Dayuuum! Maybe if I just copy them I'll get those results!" And maybe you would, at first, but then eventually people meet 'you' and then your content doesn't mesh up with who you are. Or, you finally hate trying to be someone you're not and then rebrand as yourself and have to start from scratch. You are enough just as you are. You are unique and wonderful, and the right people will love you for you. Just be you right from the start and trust you will find your voice.

- **Be consistent.** I can't stress this enough. You don't have to post 10 times a day, or even 3 times a day. Heck, you can post just once a week, BUT you better show up every week consistently to do it. Your consistency speaks to your reliability. If I'm used to you posting daily and then you disappear for a month, I'll be following someone else before you've returned. So, pick your frequency and stick to it. Not only is consistency important for cultivating a loyal following, but is also speaks to your habits, and your habits form your results in everything you do in your life. My suggestions? Make it daily, because daily habits are the ones we don't forget about that become second nature to us.
- **Make Yourself Easy to Find and Connect With.** Your handle, or username, should be the same on all platforms so I can easily look you up. If you're @ultra.unicorn.58608373636 on Instagram and

@jennytheawesome385968675 on Facebook I'll never find you on both. Pick one and use it on every platform you use, and ideally make it clean (not a word and number jumble) and easy to remember. Then link up your websites and give users the ability to e-mail you. Accessibility and ease are important in a day and age where humans now have a shorter attention spans than goldfish (I'm serious, they did a study). Make yourself easy to find and easy to get in touch with, otherwise, the average person will go to the person who has done so.

- **Dedicate to Learning Each Platform.** You don't need to use every platform, but each one you choose to use you need to take the time to learn how to use it properly. Each platform is designed to do something different in how it displays information to its users. They each have their own personality, so to speak, so make sure you're taking the time to 'speak the language' so that users love how you present your information on each platform you post on.
- **Organic Before Paid.** Dumping money into running ads on social media won't guarantee you clients, or followers, or even likes. Work on getting interaction

and followers organically first. If it works organically then it can work as a paid ad. Content and quality come first. When you're seeing good organic engagement, then you can move on to making paid ads that will resonate with your ideal clients.

What ads do you click on?

We often underestimate the power of reflecting on our own actions when doing market research. We are all consumers, but that often gets forgotten when we put on the sales hat. Think about what ads you click on online that you found irresistible, and which ones you scoffed at.

I remember talking to my dad about advertising on Facebook a while back, and I remember his reaction so clearly. He sighed, rolled his eyes, and said, "I hate those things." I didn't know what to say for a moment and then the light bulb went off in my head. My dad rarely used Facebook, barely followed anyone, and only had a couple hundred Facebook friends. Any ads that targeted him had very little data to target, so he was only getting broad advertising showing up on his feed, none of which resonated with him.

As an advertiser this is an invaluable reminder to set

parameters that ensure your ad is shown to your niche market, not just one aspect of it. In my dad's case ads were locking onto him being a male in his 50's. That's not very specific at all, and hence the ads he was seeing weren't at all interesting to him. When setting up an ad you need to ensure it takes several factors into account, and only shows the ad to people who meet all or several aspects of the criteria.

Think back to your own ad experience while on any website or social media platform and write down what comes to mind (if you can't think of anything just hop online and scroll until you come across some ads):

- What ads were a turn-off?
    - What didn't you like?
    - How did they make you feel?
    - What was the imagery?
    - What was the wording?
    - What was the subject matter?
- What ads did you like and/or click on, comment, or like?
    - What was appealing about them?
    - What was the text like?

- What type of image did they use?
- Was the subject matter something you had an interest in?

Doing this practice, you'll see very quickly what worked and why it worked, as well as what didn't and why it didn't. Landing the right ad with the right potential customer isn't blind luck, it's precision, skill, integrity, and heart. It's a learnable skill.

From now on pay attention to every ad that comes your way, and mentally break down why it did or didn't appeal to you. The more you do it, the better you'll understand how to craft your own marketing materials in a way that will resonate with your ideal clients.

Wealth Builder To-do List:

- Get behind the idea of marketing yourself, your services, goods, business, or whatever you're embarking on to do to earn money!
- Commit to educating yourself on marketing techniques and sales techniques.
- Say out loud and proud: *I market myself and my goods/services because I believe what I do has value to others!*

CHAPTER 8: MONEY MANAGEMENT

Creating various income streams is just one piece of the puzzle to accumulating riches; what you do with the money you make is the other. Some simple money management will allow you to turn money into more money, keep your savings growing, cover your expenses, and allow you the fun and joy of spending along the way.

WHAT YOU DO WITH MONEY IS AS IMPORTANT AS THE TIME AND ENERGY THAT YOU PUT INTO MAKING IT

Just like trying to hide their head in the sand about knowing their financial situation, most people veer away from managing the money they do have. That or people put it off, saying, "I'll learn how to manage money when I have some." It's a task that often comes across as long and tedious when in reality it's not difficult or time consuming to do.

The reality is, if you don't manage the money you already have, you won't be getting any more of it. Remember the Law of Attraction? Energy flows where your attention goes. That means, in order to get more money, you first need to know how to manage what you've got. It will also place your attention on money more regularly, which means you'll be attracting more of it naturally.

ACCOUNT DISPERSEMENT

Dividing up your money into separate accounts for varying intended uses may seem like an unnecessary extra step, however, it's one of the most profound things you can do to build wealth. What happens when our money is all sitting in one account? We struggle to keep our priorities straight. It sounds simple to keep savings and spending all organized in our minds, but in reality, it's not so simple.

Let's say you intend to save $100 every month, and you mentally plan to not touch that $100 (which is $200 month 2, $300 month 3, etc.). But that savings is mixed in with all your other money. You then pay your bills, unexpected expenses, dinners out, groceries, and 100 other things, from that same account. How do you keep it all straight? It becomes a mess very quickly, you forget how much you 'can't' touch, an unexpected something pops up, and bam, your account is empty.

By taking some simple steps and having just a few different accounts you move your money into for different purposes (a simple thing to do with modern online banking) you will see your money grow!

It is best to separate your incoming monies into different accounts as they come in (by paycheck) or, if you have money coming in more frequently due to various income streams, on a weekly basis. When your money comes in you'll divide it percentage wise into each account. The percent that goes into each account will depend on how much money you have left over after your necessities are deducted and will change as your income increases. Quickly reassess your percentages every quarter to make sure you're making the most of your delegated funds.

Living Expenses

You remember how we did a breakdown of expenses before? That's coming in handy as we get things set up, isn't it? Now you know your monthly living expenses and how much to delegate into this account from your incoming revenue sources! This is the account you pay the bills with, and that's all it's for. Automatic withdrawals, rent/mortgage, car payments, insurance, groceries, utilities, internet, paper products – all that stuff is covered from here.

Figure out what this percentage out of your income is needed to go into this account, and then divide up the rest into thirds. So, for example, if 70% of your income goes towards your necessities, then you have 30% left over to delegate between the next 3 accounts. This gives you 10% of your total income to divvy up evenly into each of the next three accounts.

Savings

This is the account you watch grow. The money goes in and stays in. It's not a rainy-day fund; if you prepare for a rainy day, you'll get one. This is untouchable and assures you you'll always have money.

Investments Fund

Your investment account will be used to turn your money into more money. In the next chapter, we'll get into investment options for this money.

Fun Money

All work and no play… what's the point? Your subconscious will battle you if you try to not spend a dime on anything fun and only try to save. You'll be fine for a while and then, you'll go blow a ton of money because you've been repressing your needs. It also goes against the principle of an abundance mindset to deny yourself the thing you want. This account is to be used to indulge in the things and experiences you want.

BONUS: Physical Money Jar

This last one isn't an account, but a very helpful tool in money manifesting. In a world where we all use plastic more often instead of bills and coins, money has become even more abstract. Having physical money in your environment helps you to focus on it more. Any time you have spare change, put it in the jar, and watch the jar fill up. The tangible experience is irreplaceable.

Wealth Builder To-do List:

- Open up 4 accounts to divide your earnings into: Living Expenses, Savings, Investments Fund, and Fun Money
- Have a jar for putting physical money into
- Say out loud and proud: *I manage my money so money comes to me!*

CHAPTER 9: PUTTING MONEY TO WORK

Now that we've talked about how to make money let's talk about how to use it in a way that multiplies it; let's put money to work for you! There is a multitude of ways to invest your money so that it grows. By investing you can substantially boost your net worth by multiplying the bucks you already have.

LIKE ATTRACTS LIKE

MONEY ATTRACTS MORE MONEY

Think of your money as little businessmen, apt at recruiting more businessmen to work for you. Each little guy is going to work for you, to bring on more new recruits.

STOCKS

I know a lot of people who are scared to invest in the stock market. They feel it's the same risk as gambling. While no, there are no guarantees, if you take the time to learn about the stock market, and how it works, you'll learn how to make smart investments, and to act rationally instead of emotionally.

The biggest issue with stocks is that people panic when they think they are, 1. Going to miss out, or 2. Going to lose. These impulses are what cause people to make mistakes that cost them. Warren Buffet, the world's foremost investor, has simple wisdom that anyone wanting to profit at stocks needs to live by, "Be fearful when others are greedy, and greedy when others are fearful."

As much as we'd like to think the stock market rises and falls solely based on how a company is actually doing, the truth is that it rises and falls on public opinion more often than not. If a company gets bad news in the press then the stock falls, if it gets good news the price rises, regardless of how the company is actually doing. Once you understand it's a people game as much as relying on how good a company is doing, you can better perceive the market.

There are some great practice apps out there for stocks. Download one and try playing around with it for a while to get an idea of how it works. Start researching companies and watch how their stats go up and down. Keep an eye on the press they get, as well as announcements they release, in addition to the general state of the stock market.

You can invest in stocks that pay out dividends,

invest for a long haul, or day trade. There are many ways to profit in the stock market.

Stock Tips:

- Don't invest or withdraw on impulse; remember acting on fear and/or greed will lead to ill choices.
- Diversify your investments, not just into different companies, but different business sectors. While one sector is down often others are up, giving you room to move some stock investments at any given time, without being locked in during a low in a single sector.
- Avoid fads. It's impossible to tell what will soar and what will flop.
- Focus on investing in things that people will always need; real estate, food, pharmaceuticals, banking, clothing, etc. these will always be needed for day to day life.
- Resist the temptation to buy during a *bull market*. A bull market is when the stock prices are soaring, and people and buying up stocks like crazy, driving the prices higher and higher. Instinctually people want to buy because they see the prices rising and fear that

they will indefinitely rise, so that if they don't invest right now they will miss out forever. However, there's no judging when the rise will begin to fall back toward real market value and overpaying on stocks is never a smart investment. If you invested while the stocks were lower, this is a great time to sell! Then you can buy back in when the stocks fall again with a hefty addition to your bank account in the process!

- Wait out a *bear market*. A bear market is when stock prices are falling, and most investors panic and sell off their stocks at a loss for fear of losing even more. Don't give into the panic and wait it out instead. In fact, this is a great time to invest in new stocks while they are at rock bottom prices!

REAL ESTATE

Real Estate investing is one of the smartest choices and most likely to have high ROI (Return on Investment). Real estate is most often a long game (buy and hold onto the property until the ideal time to sell) and of course, tends to demand more capital upfront to invest in. If you're currently renting, then step one is to save up for a down payment on a home for yourself. Instead of money going to rent (AKA being gone forever) by paying into a mortgage, aside from the interest rate that goes to the lending institution, it's like paying into a savings account (when you sell the house, you get the money back, wahoo!). In addition, when you go to move your house will likely have appreciated in value, giving you even more money when you sell it.

If you already own your home, investing in an investment property is a great way to use your money to create more of it. You could buy land, commercial real estate to rent out to businesses, or residential properties to rent out to individuals. Purchasing land, depending on its location, can sometimes arise with opportunities for developers to want to purchase it to build upon. And the great thing about properties you can rent out is that the extra income stream helps to cover the mortgage (and sometimes even provides a profit margin).

At the end of the day, real estate is a smart investment.

HIGH-INTEREST ACCOUNTS

Better than hiding the money under the mattress,

but how much better? That depends. Banking interest rates on savings accounts aren't what they used to be. Even high-interest rate savings accounts payouts are negligible. Most banks have somewhere between 0.5% up to about 3.0%. However, as long as they payout and allow you free access to move your money about, they can be a place to rest the money while you're deciding where else to invest it and gives you a little something in the meantime.

BUSINESSES

Private sector investments have been a growing trend. This includes investment in things such as small businesses, inventions, and entrepreneurs, that aren't on the stock market. TV shows, such as *Dragon's Den* and *Shark Tank*, have brought this type of investing into the limelight. Now, while you might not have millions lying around to invest, not every company needs that kind of capital. There are companies of all sizes that need investments to get them off of the ground.

BONDS

The simplest way to think of a bond is to think of yourself as giving a loan, with a fixed term, at a set or variable interest rate to be paid back to you at. When you invest in bonds, generally in corporate bonds or government bonds, terms are set up upfront about the duration and the interest. As with any investment, there is some risk; you can lose money by turning in the bond before maturity, or if the issuer defaults on their payments.

GOLD

You can invest in physical gold or investing in gold mining companies. While the price of gold is known to rise and fall, it's generally considered a safe investment; it's not like we're suddenly all going to decide we hate gold as a commodity for adornment after all, and even if we did, it's used in technology and medicine, among a variety of other things. In addition, gold stocks are known to have great dividend payouts, even during a low market value. It gives you another option for diversifying. Just as with stocks, it fluctuates, so if you plan to invest be sure not to buy when it's resting at a high.

GIC (Canadian)

A GIC, or Guaranteed Investment Certificate, falls into the range of a high-interest savings account. However, for the full benefit, you lock your money in for a set term and then collect your payout. I recently went to several top Canadian financial institutions websites and used their GIC calculator to see just what this would amount to in terms of investing. Setting $5000 into the GIC with a 5-year term (meaning the investor cannot touch that without penalties until the term is up) the payout would be $5387, meaning the interest made would be a meager $387 after 5 years! You can make more in a single day on the stocks if you day trade. My point being, this isn't the most prolific investment option.

YOURSELF

There's no better bet than on a person with a mission who is passionate to see it through. That person is you. You're on a mission to radically change your financial world, which in turn will demand of you to rise up to the occasion. A financial remodel in your life comes from a personal remodeling in the beliefs and mindset department.

You need an unwavering belief in yourself to make these changes, and the tools and know-how to pull it off. This makes investing in yourself the single greatest investment you can make. Put the time and the money into supporting your personal development on this journey.

Nothing Changes If Nothing Changes

It takes work to overhaul our beliefs, but that leads to incredible change. Your beliefs create your thoughts, your thoughts create your actions which bridge the non-physical and physical worlds, and your actions lead to your results. It all starts with those deep seeded beliefs.

To create change that deep takes a lot of inner reflection and reprogramming of thought and is a hell-of-a-lot easier with help. Investing in books, webinars, live seminars, coaching groups, and one on one coaching will help you through the process much faster. Outside perspective helps you to find those missing pieces, move through them, and get to the next level. What you struggle with and can't seem to figure out can be spotted and identified really quickly by a good coach, and they can tell you what you need to do next. It's all about perspective, and in the midst of our own lives, we tend not to see the forest through the trees.

You may also have an idea, or see an opportunity, to

do something to propel yourself (or your business) forward in a big way that has a big price tag. It's easy to ho-hum over it, and let fear, doubt, and worry creep in about the, "but what if it doesn't work?" Kick that thought to the curb. It'll work because you'll make it work.

Successful people aren't successful because of luck, it's because of their mindset. They don't hope it works, they get in, roll up their sleeves, and do what needs to be done to make the most of each opportunity. You're an opportunity magnet, dedicated and driven, and you're going to see it through and trust the Universe is going to have your back along the way!

Wealth Builder To-do List:

- Dedicate to putting in time to learn about investing. One by one move through the above list, make sure you understand what's involved and then start investing to make your money grow.
- Invest in yourself. You are your best bet for success.
- Say out loud and proud: *My money makes me more money!*

CHAPTER 10: MONEY HABITS

If it ain't broke, don't fix it. For some reason when people approach wealth building they feel the need to invent a new way to get rich. While, sure, a new idea or invention may be the catalyst to bring the money in for some people, the methods, mindset, and habits needed to get there have already been discovered.

YOU DON'T NEED TO RECREATE THE WHEEL

They say imitation is the most sincere form of flattery; it's also the path to wealth. If you want to get rich, it's time to follow in the footsteps of other rich people! As discussed in Chapter 5, a Morning Routine is the habit of champions. When interviewed, almost all successful people from all walks of life attest their success to a morning routine!

Crafting a Morning Routine

It's important to note there's no singular right way to have a morning routine, the activities you choose to incorporate and the order you do them in ultimately comes down to what works for you. I'd encourage you to try all of the suggested activities in this chapter before deciding yay or nay to using them daily; always remember the path to wealth is one of personal growth, so pushing outside of your comfort zone is a good thing!

HYDRATION

If you're like me when you hop out of bed in the morning the first priority is a dash to the bathroom for a big pee. Overnight our body goes through all of its restorative functions and whatever fluids went in before bed need to come out! This makes rehydrating a priority. Drinking a big glass of water (I drink 25oz upon waking) helps your body to wake up more naturally. Feeling fatigue, particularly mental fatigue, is most often a sign of dehydration. Getting hydrated right off the bat can help you to focus and tackle the rest of your morning routine with much more ease.

EXERCISE

Get your body moving! When you exercise your body wakes up very quickly. The blood begins flowing, the endorphins start pumping out, and you find yourself feeling energized and ready to take on the day. It also puts you in a better mood, and of course, a healthy body gets sick less often, so it saves you time and improves your quality of life. Grab an account through the link below to access incredible home fitness programs to incorporate into your morning routine:

www.AmandaRoseFitness.com

NUTRITION

Your brain needs fuel, and *good* fuel at that, to perform optimally. Eating in the morning kicks off your metabolism and gives your brain energy to think and process information. This is the best time of day to have a nutrient-dense meal. Personally, I don't have a big appetite in the morning, so I drink a super-food nutrition shake. It's packed with protein, antioxidants, phytonutrients, pre-biotics, probiotics, vitamins, and minerals that give my body an amazing dose of nutritional awesomeness. If you want to know what shake I use you can reach out to me for more information at: amanda@amandarosefitness.com

MEDITATION

Our mind is like a mega-supercomputer that never shuts down. Not ever. Even when we're sleeping it's busy governing our body systems and sending us dream imagery.

Giving our brains a chance to do nothing, to stop the incessant chatter of thought, is like allowing your computer to reset; after it's had a break it can process information much faster! It also puts you in tune with the Universe and allows you to receive information and ideas that you can't when your brain is busy thinking about the laundry, making dinner, getting that work report done, making a doctor's appointment, and 30 other things.

To meditate, simply find a quiet place where you won't be disturbed, then sit or lay down comfortably. Close your eyes and focus on your breath. If a thought comes up, gently push it away, and refocus on your breath. That's all there is to it.

If you feel called to do so, then you can add various elements to your practice. You could listen to a guided meditation, use essential oils or incense, hold crystals, listen to calming music, lay on a chakra mat; whatever helps you feel more connected. At its base this practice is all about the stillness of the mind, however you achieve that mental stillness is up to you.

GRATITUDE

Adding a morning gratitude practice has been one of the most profound life-changing things I've done – and it's so simple to do! We talked earlier in this book about the Law of Attraction, and how the Universe responds to your thoughts and feelings by reflecting them back to you. Gratitude puts you in a state of joy and keeps you focused on the things you love and want to attract into your life. By doing this daily, in the morning, before your day begins, you put yourself in a state of joy which will attract more things for you to be joyful about throughout your day.

You can be grateful for:

1. Things you've received (past)
2. Things you're currently receiving (present)
3. Things that are coming to you (future)

This can help you to think of the multitude of things you've received over the course of your entire life, as well as to spark your imagination about what you want to attract in your future. By being grateful for something before you receive it you guarantee it is coming to you.

There are no limits to what you can be grateful for, and the more you practice it the more you'll realize that you have to celebrate! Every day is a blessing, good health is a blessing, money is a blessing, friendship is a blessing, having time to do what you want, the taste of your favorite food, fresh flowing water; the list of things that make our lives so enjoyable is unending.

Choose 10 things every morning to give thanks for, and your life will dramatically change.

VISUALIZATION

Your imagination is your most powerful tool. The Universe reciprocates your thoughts into the physical world, and thoughts fueled by emotion are supercharged. When you visualize, in detail, the scenario you want to live as if it's real and you feel into it, you are bringing it into the physical realm.

- Get clear on what you want to manifest
- Imagine it as if it's happening now, and picture:
    - How do you get the news?
    - Who is the first person you tell?
    - Where are you?

    - How do you feel?
    - What can you sense (taste, touch, see, smell, and hear)?
    - How do you celebrate?
- By going through the above you will be able to picture it as if it's happening and feel grateful for it as if you already have it

AFFIRTMATIONS

Affirmations help to re-program your subconscious mind by replacing old negative unsupportive beliefs with new positive supportive ones. What are your goals? What 'story' do you want to rewrite? Earlier in this book we delved into the limited beliefs that we can pick up about money in our youth. Think about what came up for you then and re-write those beliefs to support who you want to become.

Some examples of money affirmations:

- I am a money magnet
- Money comes to me easily and effortlessly
- I love money and money loves me
- Money empowers me to do, be, and have the things that bring me joy

- Money is freedom
- Money is the source of great things
- I can have money and love
- I manage money with ease
- Money and I are besties
- Money and I vibrate on the same wavelength
- Money can't stay away from me

PERSONAL DEVELOPMENT

Read, listen, or watch personal development each day. This could be a book, audiobook, podcast, or video, about personal growth. Business, the law of attraction, self-help, money management, how to be a better parent, etc. the topic can change, or you may focus more in one area, but whatever you choose, work on your own personal growth journey. You're the best investment in your life, so learn, grow, change, and thrive!

JOURNALING

Journaling is such an easy thing to do with such wonderful benefits. Taking just a few minutes to write out your thoughts helps to unload your brain – all too often we can mull around the same thoughts over and over. When we write it down, it allows us to let it go, and free up some mental bandwidth. You will feel better emotionally; just as talking to someone about situations in your life is cathartic, so is writing them down. It gives you a sounding board for your thoughts and a release.

Writing also helps you to brainstorm and track your ideas. There are often so many tasks in any given day that thoughts and ideas speed in and out of our minds at 100 miles an hour. Taking the time to write down anything that stuck out will potentially lead to an idea you wish to develop down the road.

SET AN INTENTION FOR THE DAY

By taking a moment in the morning to set an intention for the day you will have given yourself a focal point for your day. This helps with purpose and efficiency in everything you do. Your intention could be a statement or a word that you use to guide your day.

Your intention word or statement will mean different things in different situations throughout the day. Let's say your intention for the day was 'Learn,' this could be learning for you, helping others learn, educating your market about your product, aiding a new employee in learning the ropes – it can also be all of those things, and more. When you set an intention the opportunities to use it throughout your day present themselves to you.

Here are some examples:

- Growth
- Learn
- Love
- Assist
- Give
- Fun
- Strength
- Structure
- Lead with Love
- Make a Difference
- Lift Others Up
- Lead by Example
- Track Success
- Celebrate Every Win

DAILY GOALS

You know what they say: *the difference between a goal and a dream is a deadline*. What can you do *today* to move closer to your ultimate goals? What would leave you feeling accomplished at the end of the day? What could you do that would take you one step closer to your goals? Think it out and write it down.

When we set a big goal, we need to reverse engineer it, so we know what needs to be done in a year, a quarter, a month, a week, and a day to make sure that goal is achieved. This plays a part in your daily goals. What's the big thing you're aiming to achieve and what can you do today to progress towards it?

TO DO LIST

Last, but not least, putting together a to-do list gives your day structure, helps you get more done, keeps you on track, and declutters your brain. You can do a written list or use an app – but make a list. As you get things done throughout the day you check them off the list and can see visible progress. It can also help you to avoid wasting vast amounts of time continuously trying to decide what needs to be done next. Get organized so you can knock it out of the park!

Wealth Builder To-do List:

- Try out the morning routine activities. Pick a morning to get up and try all of the activities above (1-2 hours should be enough to get them all done) and see which ones resonate with you. If you love them all you can use them all. If not, pick your favorites and craft your own morning routine.
- Say out loud and proud: *My morning routine sets me up for success with money and all of my endeavors!*

CHAPTER 11: THE MONEY VIBRATION

Everything in the Universe is energy, and all energy vibrates. Therefore, there is a money vibration, and you just have to get on it to attract money into your life through the Law of Attraction. So, what frequency does money vibrate on? The answer might surprise you...

THE FREQUENCY OF LOVE IS THE FREQUENCY OF MONEY

Yes, that's right. You attract money through the awesome power of love! Love is the key that opens up the doors to manifesting everything your heart desires.

As we earlier discussed, we manifest through our thoughts and our feelings. Your thoughts are fueled by your emotions, so the stronger the emotion, the more intensely you will magnetize what you're thinking about to you. And there is no stronger emotion than love.

This works both ways; if you're thinking about money while feeling anger about your bills, jealous of someone else's wealth, hate for the need for money, or depressed about how empty your bank account is, your vibrational frequency is attracting more circumstances around money for you to feel anger, jealousy, hate, and depression about. On the flip side when you feel grateful for the services provided to you that your bills represent, happy for the person who is wealthy, love for money and its place in your life, and joy for receiving money in any denomination, then your vibration will attract more circumstances around money for you to feel grateful, happy, joyful, and love for!

Get on the Vibration of Love
For it is the Key
To Everything Your Heart Desires

This is the simplest way to use the Law of Attraction, and quite possibly the most powerful. If you can be happy *now* and feel love *now* for what you want as if you already have it, it will come to you. You'll find life is a joy, that your dreams come to pass one by one, and that the struggles melt away.

We are feeling beings, and this is not to say you will never feel hate or anger, or resentment, or sadness, or any other lower energy emotion. The point is not to live in the negativity. Be aware of your emotional state and get onto a positive vibrational emotion as quickly as you can. In every situation there is something to be grateful for, you just need to find it.

> "LET US RISE UP AND BE THANKFUL,
>
> FOR IF WE DIDN'T LEARN A LOT AT LEAST WE LEARNED A LITTLE,
>
> AND IF WE DIDN'T LEARN A LITTLE, AT LEAST WE DIDN'T GET SICK,
>
> AND IF WE GOT SICK, AT LEAST WE DIDN'T DIE;
>
> SO, LET US ALL BE THANKFUL."
>
> **-BUDDHA**

FEAR & DOUBT

What takes us out of a state of love & trust, and gathers up all of the reasons why it won't work? Fear & doubt are the culprits.

To give love for all you have, and all you want to receive, comes from faith that what you have will continue to be there and that what you want will come. It is to believe in the Universe, to know the unseen energy has your back and is moving energetically to match you. You get what you give. Give love for what you want, and the law says you must receive it.

But... what if it doesn't come? What if I'm stuck? What if I can't (fill in the blank)? *Insert panic and fear here.* These feelings of fear and doubt crop up from those old unsupportive beliefs we picked up in our youth. It is through the process of releasing these thoughts and returning to love that we can grow out of fear and doubt, learn to trust, and watch the magic of life unfold before us.

This is where continual person growth comes into play. We have to keep growing and learning; it comes from practice. Your dream life won't just appear in a puff of smoke, it will move towards you as you get into energetic alignment with it. That requires continually refocusing on what you want. During any given day we think umpteen bazillion thoughts about so many different things, both little and big, that we can't even remember it all. Refocusing on your goals, on what you want to attract, and how you want to feel, is the key.

The Universe presents to you, throughout every day, a plethora of possibilities for your life; all of it is yours for the taking, you simply must give love. See someone driving your dream car? Instead of falling into jealousy, feel happy for the person, and feel love for the car! You will magnetize it to you! See a new mom with a baby when you've been trying to conceive? Feel joy and love for babies! See a friend get hired for their dream job? Feel thankful and give love for dream jobs!

See something you don't want in your life? Then don't give it an emotional reaction, just turn away from it. Remember it is your thoughts fueled by emotions that attract those things into your life! By not giving an emotional response you avoid magnetizing it to you.

THE DREAM

I had the most interesting dream last night. It was intense, and any other day it would have been a nightmare. It was so utterly symbolic of how fear and doubt hold us back, and the choices we have to either give in to ear and doubt *or* tell fear and doubt to bugger off because we are ready to live large and in charge!

I dreamt that I had been kidnapped, and by the end of it, the kidnapper was ready to kill me. In my dream, the kidnapper represented my own fear and doubt. I saw 3 options; die, run, or fight back. I fought back and took out my attacker, AKA I killed my fear and doubt, so it no longer had any hold over me.

When I woke up, unlike waking from a nightmare, I didn't feel disturbed by the dream. I felt *free*. I felt freer than I'd felt in... quite possibly ever. The dream was a metaphor for my limiting beliefs holding me back from living my dream life. The kidnapper was my fear and my doubt incarnate, and in my dream, I killed it and freed myself. It was cathartic.

KILL 'EM

What fears and doubts are holding you back? When you think about living the life you've always wanted to live, what *"ifs, ands,* or *buts,"* jump out. Write them all down on a piece of paper. Be thorough and take as much time as you need to get them out.

Once you have them written out, set the piece of paper on fire (be safe, have a big metal or glass bowl to place the paper in while it burns) and as it burns, and the smoke rises, visualize those fears dissipating into nothingness. You've killed them, and now you're free to move forward.

Wealth Builder To-do List:

- Love is the key to all the wealth, joy, and happiness you want. Lead with love.
- Write out all of your fears and doubts on a piece of paper and then burn them. Set yourself free.
- Say out loud and proud: *I love money and my energy is in alignment with money!*

CHAPTER 12: PUTTING IT ALL TOGETHER

We've covered a lot of ground in this book; from the importance of mindset to incorporating Law of Attraction, and the actionable steps to generate income and grow your money. It's a lot of information all in one fell swoop. Knowledge is power for change, but *only* when we put it into practice. In this chapter, we're going to recap everything we've learned and set an action plan for making it a new part of your life!

WHAT LIMITING BELIEFS DO YOU HAVE ABOUT MONEY?

Knowing how you feel deep down to your core about money is the first step to change. Take the time to investigate your belief system. Ask the questions that drum up the answers, even if it's tough, because until our foundational beliefs change, our financial situation isn't going to change.

PLANT NEW BELIEFS

Once you're clear about what beliefs you have picked up about money as you grew up, you can release them, and then plant some new seeds. Who do you want to become? What do you want to accomplish? What supportive beliefs do you need to believe in order to get there?

WHAT MONEY REALLY IS

Keep reminding yourself that money is a blank slate. It's an I.O.U. for whatever you want to put it towards. It isn't inherently good or bad. Money is the conduit for you to be, do, and have all of the things that bring you joy in life.

THE UNIVERSE AND YOU

You're not on this transformative journey alone. The Universe is always there with you, it's there supporting you every step of the way. Keep in mind your thoughts become your physical reality, so take stock often about what you're thinking, how you're feeling, and readjust so you're constantly back in alignment with attracting what you truly want into your life. Gratitude is the key!

FINANCIAL CLARITY

Not knowing your financial situation doesn't make it better. you can't move forward, make changes, and create financial freedom when you're wandering around in the dark. Take the time to investigate your financial situation. Understand where you're at and then take action to create positive change.

MONEY MANAGEMENT

Energy flows where your attention goes; start focusing on managing your money now. Set up the accounts, get a money jar, and begin delegating your current funds proportionately. As you begin to manage the money you do have, you are showing the Universe you know how to handle money, so it can send more of it your way!

INCOME

Keep in mind that *working income* is only one piece of the puzzle and that financial freedom requires *passive income* streams. While you're making working income, invest the time to start getting passive income streams set up. The options for creating passive income are plentiful so you can find one or more you really enjoy. They are worth the effort in the long run, generating money for you even while you sleep!

INVESTING

Turn your money into more money. Carve out some time to learn about investments in an area you're interested in, and then implement it. This will grow your net worth exponentially.

MINDSET

Wealth is a mindset. Your personal growth is paramount to creating the life you've always wanted to live. An upgrade to the bank account requires an upgrade in the mind. Surround yourself with successful people, personal development books, audio recordings, hire a coach – do whatever you need to do to grow. It's not what you need to do, but who you have to become, to be abundant.

SUCCESSFUL HABITS

Our habits define our results. What we do on a day to day basis adds up to big results over time. To be successful, we need to incorporate successful habits in our daily lives. Craft a morning routine using the habits successful people do and stick to it to transform your life and your finances.

ENERGETIC ALIGNMENT

Everything in the Universe is vibrating at an energetic frequency, including money. Money is vibrating at the frequency of love. Use gratitude as a tool to bring your thoughts to those of happiness and love to regularly get onto the frequency of love.

Wealth Builder To-do List:

- If you haven't already, begin to implement everything you've learned
- Over the next 7 days follow *A Week of Money Manifesting Practices* to incorporate Law of Attraction with a focus on abundance into your daily life
- Say out loud and proud: *I am great with money; money loves me and I love money!*

A Week of Money Manifesting Practices

Day 1: Money Gratitude

Nothing draws money to you faster than a grateful heart. How you feel when you think about money is the single most important factor when it comes to making it and keeping it. If you feel anxiety, anger, depression, worry, or doubt about money, more circumstances will present themselves for you to continue to feel that way. By changing how you feel now, you'll create a new future for positive money experiences.

If you are not Grateful for What You Already Have

You Cannot Receive More

Today's practice is a 3-prong approach to making yourself a money magnet! By giving thanks for all the money you've received in your past, all the money you're receiving now, and all of the money you'll be receiving in the future, you are supercharging yourself to get in alignment with the vibration of money!

PAST

As children, we don't think about money because it is paid for us by others. But money was a big part of our existence right from day one! Money was needed for the doctors, and the hospital, to buy the diapers, and the baby clothes, and the vaccinations, among a multitude of other things! As you grew you constantly needed new clothing for your changing body. Food, water, shelter, toys, an education; it doesn't take much digging to see how many things were provided for you that cost money to help you grow and flourish! Think through your childhood and adolescence and write down at least 10 things that were provided to you as you grew that cost money, and one by one say 'thank you' for each!

PRESENT

Just take a look around your home or dwelling and you'll see very quickly how many things you've attracted to you that cost money! Do you have electricity? Running water? Heat? A roof over your head? Clothes? Shoes? Electronics? Furniture? Food in the fridge? Entertainment? Toiletries? All of these things cost money!

What are the last 5 ways money came to you? Write down at least 5 things money is providing for you currently and the last 5 ways money arrived in your life, and then read through the lists and say 'thank you' for each!

FUTURE

Giving thanks for the money that's yet to arrive is one of the most powerful things you can do. It is you telling the Universe that you believe it will show up, that you trust the process, and have faith it's on its way. You do not need to know the 'how' – in fact, you cannot know 'how.' *How* it will come to you is the domain of the Universe; your job is all about believing and trusting that it will come.

Money has always shown up for you throughout your life, you wouldn't be alive to read this otherwise, so you know it's going to show up again in the future. Use this affirmation to give thanks for everything that's on its way to you: "Thank you, thank you, thank you for all of the abundance in my life and all that is coming to me! Money comes to me easily and effortlessly! I am a money magnet, and money is all around me!"

Next, write out a list of 10 things you'll use money to buy in the future (think big!) and say thank you for each thing on that list as if you've already received them!

Day 2: Magnetic Money

We live in a world where our money is primarily digital, and our wallets are full of more plastic than physical money. This is incredibly convenient, giving us access to money at all times, however, it's more like having a key or access card to get to money, not money itself.

Like attracts like. So, having some physical money around will draw more money to you. The denomination itself is irrelevant, it's the physical money that matters. Keep a dollar bill (or for my fellow Canadians a loonie) in your wallet at all times. This is a beacon to attract more bills and coins into your wallet! In addition, every time you open your wallet you'll see money, it'll never be empty, and that will help to strengthen your belief and faith that money is always there for you!

MONEY MAGNET HOME

One of my favorite practices in the *penny in every corner* money magnet practice! It's so simple, and yet supercharges your home to be a wealth magnet! Simply take a bunch of pennies and put them in every corner of every room in your house. This takes about 5-10 minutes, depending on the size of your home, and will leave you feeling empowered when you're done!

Imagine as you place each penny down that they are sending out a magnetic field, drawing more money to them (they really are!). With each one you put down the magnetic field that's drawing money to your home is getting stronger and stronger. Each room you complete becomes a wealth beacon, signaling to the Universe that money exists here, and to send more!

Picture in your mind, once all the pennies are set, that they are sending energy to each other, in a line across the floor, like a white light, connecting them all. With them being in every corner they are outlining the entire room in their magnetic energy! Picture your whole home bathed in this white light, like a beacon to the Universe, sending a magnetic signal for more money to come and hang out in your home!

*If you have pets or children who will move the pennies (or any risk of them trying to eat them) place them up and out of reach (for example in a kitchen you might place it in an upper corner cabinet, and in a living room on top of a bookshelf). If they can't go 100% in the corner, that's OK, just get them as close as possible.

Day 3: More Than Money

Money is the means to an end. Manifesting money for monies sake is... rather dull. It's just paper and coins. It's hard to get really excited for paper and coins, but when you think about what you'd use that money for, *that's exciting*! And because your thoughts are fueled by your emotions, it's a more powerful way to draw what you want to you!

It also opens up possibilities for various ways of receiving when you focus on your end goal, and not the money itself. For example, let's say you want to do an extravagant beach vacation. By picturing the vacation and focusing on it then it can come to you in many ways. You could win a contest, have it gifted to you, a massive discount could pop up making it affordable, someone you know could have it booked and have to cancel and give you the tickets, you could have a windfall of money to cover it; the possibilities of how it could appear are endless!

PICTURE THE END RESULT

The only question you need to answer is, "What do I want the money for?" If you've been wanting to manifest $10,000, then get clear on what that $10,000 is for. If you just picked an arbitrary number, take a step back, think about what you really want, then investigate how much it really costs. For example, if you want to buy a nice house, start browsing online, find one you love, then figure out the mortgage down payment and monthly costs. Going through this process as if you're buying what you want tells the Universe that it's real and you're making it happen. Then the Universe will move to support you in that endeavor. Browsing the house, seeing the photos, heck, call up the real estate agent for a walkthrough; the more real it is to you and the more you can picture yourself living there, means it will manifest fast!

This process works for anything. If you've been wanting money to pay off credit card debt, picture the debt at $0, write a check in the full amount you owe and place it somewhere you'll see it often and imagine how good it will feel to turn over that check to pay it off!

It doesn't matter if you want to fund starting your own business, travel, to buy any physical object, get debt free, fund a hobby; whatever it is you want all you need to do is picture the end result in as much detail as possible and be grateful as if you have it now. Take 5 minutes to do that right now!

Day 4: Make Room

What happens when you clean out a closet? It's like it suddenly turns into a super-duper high-powered vacuum that sucks everything it can into it like a vortex. In no time at all, it's full again! Clean off your desk? Same thing, piles of paper, pens, paperclips, you name it and it gets attracted there. The last time I cleaned out my purse it lasted about all of 8 seconds before, in the blink of an eye, it was full again.

Nature Abhors a Vacuum

This same phenomenon can be intentionally used to attract money! Create a space for it so it can come to you. Do this mentally, physically, and digitally, and watch the money pour in!

MENTALLY MAKE SPACE

Most people have a mental ceiling on their income. This is one of those things that can fall under the unsupportive beliefs we discussed early on in this book. They've come to believe that X amount is what they're worth, and they always level out at the amount. Sure, sometimes they come into money, and sometimes they run into financial issues, but overall, they hover around the number they've mentally got locked in.

Before money can come and stick around we have to remove the mental limits and make space for it. After going through this book and understanding money better, a lot of those old unsupportive beliefs should be loosened up at this point. Perhaps it was fear with what to do with large amounts of money, fear of being judged, fear of high taxation; whatever the case may be, you have a better understanding of what to do to make more money and keep it now.

Close your eyes a picture in your mind a large container, with a wide base, and an opening at the top. This is your mental money capacity. It's how much you'll allow to come to you. So how much fits in that container? You set that number.

Let's say on average you've been earning $30,000 a year. That's the comfort number you hover around. Imagine now that container has room for $40,000. Picture it ¾ full with $30,000 and the rest of the space is empty, and waiting to be filled.

Keep coming back to this mental exercise and keep raising the number on the container and take the time to visualize where your current amount rests so you can see all of the room waiting to be filled. Get excited about that space being there, being available for more money to come and hang out!

MAKE A PHYSICAL SPACE

You know what happens when you set aside a money jar? It attracts money. It's a very simple yet very powerful tool to build more wealth. While you can use any jar, a clear glass jar is great because you are regularly looking at the money and reminding yourself of abundance. It will continue to attract money and fill up before your eyes!

Get a jar and set it aside for money. Kick it off by adding a few coins to magnetize more money to that spot. Every time you see that jar imagine it filling up; it will in no time!

MAKE DIGITAL SPACE

With most of our banking online, opening up a new account online through your banking institute is a great way to tell the Universe to send you some money to fill up that account! Picture what the account will be for and how much money it will hold. Some accounts have a minimum amount to start gaining interest, and if that's the case, use that baseline as the image for the money you'll attract to fill the account with!

Day 5: Money All Around Me

Everything you can do to support a money positive mindset helps and this next practice is a great opportunity to teach your brain to believe your affirmations that money is all around you. We're going to literarily – you guessed it – put money all around you!

Today we're going to put money throughout your home. This is going to reinforce the idea that money is all around you, and that all you have to do is reach out and grab it at any time! This is the Universal truth, but all too often we get caught up in our present physical reality, which is actually a projection of our past mental reality. We have to shift our present mindset to create an abundant future. By engraining this new belief that money is all around you, you'll begin to really believe it, and the Universe will provide it!

MONEY SURROUNDS ME

This is similar to the penny practice, but different mentally. Depending on your current financial situation you'll need to determine the quantity and denomination you'll use, and you may add more over time if you can only do a little now. Do what you can with $1 and/or $5-dollar bills and stash them away throughout your house. In books, in a vase, in a coat pocket, on a shelf, in a desk drawer; get creative and put it all around.

At least once a day, it can be part of your morning practice, close your eyes and imagine all of this money surrounding you! Money is all around you, just waiting for you to reach out and grab it! Use the mantra, "Money is always all around me!"

Say it. Believe it. Live it!

Day 6: Magical Check

One of the manifestation stories that always stuck out to me and that made me smile and deeply believe in the process was Jim Carrey's story. Growing up in the 1990s when his comedic films were all the rage and his career was taking off, he became an actor and performer I admired greatly. Years and years later when I heard his 'rags to riches' story I was impressed on a whole new level.

First of all, if you never saw his interview on the Oprah show, there are clips online, just search for it and watch it. It's absolutely incredible. This story is a testament to the power of visualization.

When Jim Carrey was dirt poor and having a hard time getting by, he would take time every night to drive up to this spot overlooking Hollywood and imagined directors and producers having interest in his work and getting the big roles he wanted. He said this made him feel better. This is such an important takeaway; not only was he visualizing what he wanted but he was feeling it. We attract through emotion, so this is huge!

Jim wrote a check to himself for $10,000,000 for acting services rendered and dated it a few years into the future. He put it in his wallet and would take it out and look at it and know that the money and the opportunity were out there, he believed it *was* there for him, he just didn't have it yet. As the date closed in Jim Carrey landed his role on *Dumb and Dumber* for which he was paid 10 million dollars!

Some important things from this story:

- Jim did visualization and it made him feel good; the feeling good part is huge! That's the vibrational alignment that will supercharge the vision
- Jim wrote the check and carried it around as a reminder the money was on its way to him
- Jim didn't just visualize and write the check, he worked towards his dream in the meantime; believe it, visualize it, and take action, then the Universe can present the opportunities for making it happen

WRITE YOUR MAGIC CHECK

What's your passion? What gift do you want to share with the world? What do you want to get paid for it? Get clear on what you want to be & do and the money you're attracting in return for sharing your gifts with the world. Then write yourself a check for that amount and in the comments part say what it's for. Stick that in your wallet and every time you see it remember the money is on its way! Commit to visualizing that you're living it out daily and feel into it. Take action towards making this happen, while staying open to cues from the Universe for guidance.

Day 7: Happy Money

Nothing attracts money more than happiness. When you're happy, and giving love for your life, and everything in it, you become a magnet for more things you love; money, relationships, health, and all the other good things! When you come from love, the magnetic field of your body radiates at that frequency, and as we know, what you give out you must receive back multiplied!

Giving gratitude and feeling joyful about any part of your life automatically makes you attract more good things in all areas of your life. For this practice, however, we're going to be focusing in on giving good feelings for money specifically. Money all too often feels like a source of tension and sadness for most people; if you can change that so you feel good about money, you will always manifest more!

THANK YOU FOR THE MONEY FOREVER

There is more than enough abundance in the Universe to meet your needs and beyond; it is boundless! We are the only ones who limit our own income. Getting out of our own way allows the energy to flow, and the funds to grow!

This practice is a life-long commitment; anytime anything money related comes to your attention your job is to be thankful for the money! It doesn't matter if it's coming in (you get paid, finding a coin on the street, getting a gift, etc.) or going out (paying bills, buying something, giving money, etc.) your job is to feel gratitude!

Picture the money that is going out to pay for things like bills, mortgage, car payments, gifts, etc. going to other people. Imagine how happy they will feel receiving their paycheck, and how much good that money does. Think about all of the services and goods you are receiving in exchange for that money. Know that the money you give will come back to you exponentially and thank the Universe for all the money that's on its way to you!

For your paycheck, and income streams, money you find, money that's gifted, coupons, discounts, and anything else coming to you that makes you richer and saves you money, be grateful for it no matter the denomination. Any money that shows up for you is a sign you are attracting abundance! Feel gratitude even for the penny found on the sidewalk, for that is the Universe reminding you to feel happy and thankful to continue to receive more!

If at first a negative feeling comes up, such as "This paycheck is so small," "I'm so broke," "I wish I had more money," or anything else along those lines stop yourself as quick as you can and finish this sentence, "But I have to say I'm so incredibly grateful for ___________." That is your lifeline to get your thoughts back to the positive!

Let this practice become your new way of life, and your finances will be forever changed!

RESOURCES

In the following pages you will find incredible resources to help you to continue your personal growth & financial freedom journey! You will find a variety of products services that will help to build on everything you've learned in this book. Everything from supporting your spiritual and mindset growth, to hands on practical ways to create passive income, manage your finances, and build wealth! Each one of these businesses are mindset oriented.

PERSONAL GROWTH:

- Live Your Dream in Panama
- Golden Elixir Chai
- Tree Star
- Enchanted Essence
- Nobody Greater Inc.
- Kemetic Mindfulness

FINANCIAL SERVICES:

- Practical Boss Babe
- Chelsea Scomak Conte Wealth Advisor

PASSIVE INCOME CREATION:

- Get Published Workshop
- Proofing You Write
- Dan McCutcheon Book Cover Design
- Soulful Communications
- A Sparkle of Health and Beauty
- Fire Fury Fitness

Anika Wilson
NBG.as.me

Get Published Workshop

Get step-by-step guidance through the entire process from idea to finished book! From concept development, story structure, and writing habits for success, to editing, formatting, book cover, copywriting, publishing, and finally how to market your book so that it sells - this course will teach you everything you need to succeed!

Book BONUS:
Save $49.99 with Coupon Code:
MANIFESTINGMONEY

www.udemy.com/get-published-workshop

Soulful Communications

Soulful & Conscious

Copywriter | Communications Coach

Elevating The Way Women Communicate in Business

Join us at: **The Copywriting Coach Group** on f

For more details on copywriting and 1:1 coaching opportunities,

Contact: **SamanthaHaddad84@Gmail.com**

CHELSEA SCOMAK | CONTE WEALTH ADVISORS

Contact: CSCOMAK@CONTEWEALTH.COM

A Sparkle of Beauty and Health

I started my journey into "A Sparkle of Beauty and Health" as a full-time working momma to three sparkling children! As a mother, I have found passion to share my experiences and show my children dreams can come true. Just throw some glitter on it, stay in the mindset, and you guessed it: Sparkle!

Now, Sparkling is work.

You have to put time, work, and dedication, but if you are serious then Contact me and let me help put some Sparkle into your life. Invest in yourself now to create the future you desire.

Visit:

www.sarahbettencourt.com

About the Author

Amanda Rose is an avid reader and storyteller. Working in a variety of mediums and genres, communicating new ways of thinking is her passion.

Amanda works as an online Health and Fitness coach, Law of Attraction Coach, Actor, Model, Motivational Speaker, and Writer. Residing in Kingston, Ontario, with her husband and 3 cats, Amanda is currently working on her next novel. Get in touch with Amanda by visiting her website, **www.AmandaRoseFitness.com**

Author's Other Works

- Manifesting Your Best Life
- Manifesting on Purpose
- Get Published Workbook
- The Orgasmic Cookbook
- Fire Fury Freedom
- Fire Fury Frontier
- The Impending End
- A Strange Dream

Manifesting Your Best Life:

How to Stop Wishing for Change and Start Living Your Best Life

Manifesting Your Best Life Book Description:

Stop dreaming about a better life and start living it!

Manifesting You Best Life is going to show you that "Living Your Best Life" isn't just some cute meme on social media – it can be your way of life! The 21 nugget-of-wisdom chapters in this self-help book are for people who want to start living their best life, but don't know where to begin. It will give you the skills to take you from dreaming about your best life, to making it your reality!

You will learn:
•How to Identify what living your best life really means to you.
•The steps needed to stop wishing and start living your best life.
•How to use the Law of Attraction to support your efforts.
•Successful habits that will change your life.
•And how to create the life you've always wanted... And start living it NOW!

By the end of Manifesting Your Best Life, you will have a clear picture of what your dream life looks like, how to get there, and the tools and skills to make it into your reality! Are you ready to begin?

AVAILABLE ON AUDIBLE

Manifesting on Purpose:

A 3 Week Guide to Transforming Your Life Through the Law of Attraction

Manifesting on Purpose Book Description:

It's time to take manifesting off auto-pilot, get behind the wheel, and start steering your life in the direction you want it to go!

Manifesting on Purpose clarifies why we manifest what we do, why we experience the same things over and over again, until we step in and weed out our own mental gardens.

Ever wonder how is it that 2 people can start off with the same opportunity, and one will become a massive success, while the other barely scrapes by? What's the defining factor?

What do successful people know that we're missing? We've been taught that the harder we work the more money, happiness, and success we'll have in life; but if this was the case successful people would constantly we run ragged, and be bleary eyed from lack of sleep, instead of enjoying lots of free time pursuing their heart's desires. So, what are we missing?

The Law of Attraction is always working, even when we're not focused on it. The Law of Attraction states that, "Like Attracts Like," we are all energy, so our thoughts get reflected back to us. Your thoughts create your physical reality. The problem? We're always thinking! Our thoughts, ungoverned, bounce around from idea to idea, and all too often, focus on the immediate problems in our lives, creating a feedback loop. Since we attract back what we think about, if we're focused on our problems, what's going to show up? More problems!

Your mind is your most valuable asset. Your thoughts literally create your reality. Your current situation is a reflection of your previous thoughts.
Most people, however, do not consciously decide what they want, their subconscious belief systems run everything on auto-pilot; making most people feel as if they are victims of their circumstances.

YOU ARE NOT A VICTIM OF CIRCUMSTANCE!

You are in the driver's seat, you simply have to take control of the wheel! Take manifesting off auto-pilot and create the life you want!
"But I think positive thoughts," you say. Your conscious thoughts will always be secondary to your subconscious thoughts in the way of manifestation. Until you change your core beliefs to line up with who you wish to become, and what you wish to do, you cannot break the old cycles.

Are you ready to take control? Have abundance in money, love, health, freedom, experiences, and all other areas of your life? Then let's get started!

Get Published Workbook

Get Published Workbook Book Description:

Most people have thought about publishing a book, but the majority will never even begin writing one. Why? The process can seem daunting.

Conceptualizing, writing, editing, formatting, copywriting, publishing, and finally marketing; it can seem like an overwhelming amount of work when you aren't sure what each step entails.

In this workbook, you're going to learn all of my best practices so you can go from concept to published in 2-6 months pending on the length and style of your book, with full knowledge of what to expect, and what to do, so nothing will stand in your way of becoming a successful author!

Self-publishing is an incredible avenue to get your work to your readers fast, with widespread distribution, that allows you to take the lion's share of the profits for the book you put all the work into creating!

With self-publishing, you're in control, but that also means you are in charge of your own marketing campaign. Don't let that scare you away! With social media and online sales booming, you can reach your ideal reader audience easier, and at much less cost, than with traditional marketing. You just need to learn how!

Through this book, you're going to learn...

•How to brainstorm and develop a concept
•How to effectively begin writing your book
•How to create disciplined habits to finish your book
•How to edit, format, and polish your book so it's ready for publication
•Why reviews are the life-blood of self-publishing, and how to get them
•How to write an effective book description
•How to write a gripping back cover
•Why your book cover is your most important investment
•How the self-publishing process works
•Best practices for ultimate exposure
•How to use inexpensive pay-per-click campaigns to drive traffic
•Social Media Marketing
•Free marketing practices
•Inexpensive marketing options
•Importance of an author web site to boost SEO
...And much more!

It's time to write your book!

The Orgasmic Cookbook

The Orgasmic Cookbook Book Description:

Nutrition Meets Flavor.

Just because it's healthy doesn't mean it should be boring. In *The Orgasmic Cookbook* Amanda teaches her best tips and tricks to make healthy food pop with flavor! Having lost over 100 pounds Amanda knows the importance of eating healthy. As a food lover she's made it her mission to create healthy recipes packed with rich taste!

Get ready for mouth-watering recipes that will give you a whole new appreciation for food!

Fire Fury Freedom

"A veritable saga of a dystopian novel by an author with a genuine flair for detailed originality, and narrative driven storytelling, "Fire Fury Freedom" by Amanda Rose is an extraordinary and truly memorable read from cover to cover." ***-Midwest Book Review***

Prequel to the Fire Fury Frontier Series

Fire Fury Freedom Book Description:

A dying planet on the verge of collapse.... tormented pasts that haunt the present... an ancient hidden magick...

The C.D.F.P. mega-corporation rules all, with unchecked power, and dark secrets...

The planet is dying, and they are the last hope to save it... Mack, an ex-soldier of the C.D.F.P. military division, and his mercenaries, standalone against the C.D.F.P. (AKA the Company), in the fight for humanities survival. Left unchallenged, the company has ruled over the East Green Continent with an iron fist for decades. The pollution they've caused has devastated the planet, destroying the ozone, and killing off plant and animal life.

Outside of domed cities the air is thin, and the sun scorches all; it's a veritable wasteland. In the past two decades the planet has reached entirely new levels of decay. Extreme weather patterns, and massive quakes, ravage the land.

Time is running out...

Mack and his mercenary troupe set out on a quest to stop the C.D.F.P. once and for all, and the planet will test them to their limits... But are they ready for the horrors they'll uncover? Can they alone stand up against the all-powerful C.D.F.P.?

Fire Fury Frontier

"It's Mass Effect Meets Star Wars in this Harrowing Space Opera!" – BETA READER

Fire Fury Frontier Book Description:

One ship, one last chance to survive...

Humanity's home world has been destroyed from extensive global warming. For over two hundred years the last remaining humans have lived in space aboard a single massive ship, the Saisei. After generations in space, living aboard a ship is all anyone has ever known.

But space is an inhospitable home.

The ship is old and damaged, rations are low, and a planet fit for colonization has never been found.

In the vast expanse of space, as the Saisei makes way to resupply their ship, they stumble upon a discovery that will change the course of human history forever.

The Impending End

The Impending End Book Description:

It's 2005. Ayla Jefferson is 17, incredibly intelligent, sensitive, imaginative, and thoughtful. She's also contemplating suicide...

After a life long battle with mental illness plaguing her every move, Ayla is ready for death. Eerily calm, she says her goodbyes, and sets out to commit her final act.

But despite her stubborn conviction, life isn't as easy to let go of as she expected. Her hyper-imagination blurs reality and she finds herself getting lost in gripping memories. Mentally disengaged, Ayla's experiences are surreal, and discerning fact from fiction becomes harder and harder.

As the life she's so eager to leave behind begs to hold on, will she be able to leave it all behind?

A Strange Dream

Anthology of Short Stories and Poetry

A Strange Dream Book Description:

Death, Depression, Insomnia, Prostitution, Eating Disorders, Abortion, Convicts, Insanity, and Marital issues... This anthology of short stories and poetry explores the dark reaches of the mind and mental health issues.

The 9 short stories, including award winning EGGS and OUTSIDER, as well as runner up in the Canadian Writer's Guild Short Prose competition, DROWNING IN SILENCE, and 9 poems, take us on a journey from the surreal to the mundane. From day-to-day life to fantasy, the characters and situations explore many walks of life.

28863638R00108

Printed in Great Britain
by Amazon